Harry and Cheryl Salem are incredible examples of living by faith during the good times and the bad times. Even when their hearts are breaking, they trust in the Lord's unfailing love. May God continue to bless their lives and their ministry.

**—Don Nickles**
U.S. Senator, Oklahoma

Harry and Cheryl Salem are the kind of people who, even if you don't see them as often as you'd like, you can still count on the fact that they are "with" you and praying for you every step of the way. They are as responsible as anyone else is in the development of my professional career. When our son was ill, they were some of the first ones to come and pray for him. My wife and I had the privilege to meet their daughter Gabrielle at the Salems' home during my interviewing for the head coaching position at Oral Roberts University. We were also at the home-going service for Gabrielle, and we watched the grieving process that followed. The Salems have a secret to going on and winning in life that is unbeatable. We highly endorse *From Grief to Glory* because we have seen the Salems' joy and the journey that took them to that joy. *From Grief to Glory* will encourage you to discover ways to press toward victory just as the Salems have.

**—Bill Self (and wife Cindy)**
Head Coach, Men's Basketball
University of Kansas

Having known Cheryl Salem for more than twenty years and having been friends with the entire Salem family for many years, we love and appreciate Harry and Cheryl's stamina to push through their grief. This new book, *From Grief to Glory*, is the continuing courageous journey *"through the valley of the shadow of death,"* never stopping, never doubting, and never blaming God. We have watched as the Salems have come in faith to a place that is beyond our comprehension with the glory of God leading them. They truly are examples of miraculous understanding with heavenward eyes and eternal vision. As you read, they can help you find your way through grief to a restored place of God's glory!

**Gavin MacLeod (and wife Patti)**
Actor (career includes notable roles such as Murray Slaughter on *The Mary Tyler Moore Show* and Captain Merrill Stubing on *The Love Boat*)

The Scripture that comes to mind when I think of what Harry and Cheryl Salem have gone through with the loss of their daughter is *"when I am weak, then I am strong."* Harry and Cheryl let themselves be vulnerable to God and let Him do His mighty work. They were the definition of grace as they rested in His will for their daughter's life. I hope that many will learn to call on God's mighty strength in troublesome situations through this book.

**—Kim Alexis**
Model (career includes appearances on more than five hundred magazine covers)

I have known the Salems for many years. In the early years, Cheryl encouraged many who watch *The 700 Club* by giving her miraculous healing testimony. She and Harry later appeared on the show to share with our audience after the home-going of their precious daughter, Gabrielle—appearing not with the outcome that they wanted, but with the ministry God has given them. This ministry is not the one they would have chosen, but rather the one that God chose for them, birthed out of tragedy.

They are an inspiration to those who have faced the fire and experienced trials but continue on, never questioning God. Theirs is a story of trust, of commitment, of spiritual fortitude for all the world to see.

**—Pat Robertson**
Founder and Chairman,
Christian Broadcasting Network Inc.
Founder, President, and Chancellor,
Regent University
Host, *The 700 Club*

As a mother, my heart broke for my friends Cheryl and Harry Salem as I watched them have to deal with the death of their precious daughter. In the midst of indescribable loss, their faith rose up and directed us all to trust the faithful, perfect love of our heavenly Father. What the enemy meant for evil, God has worked for good as He has taken the Salems from grief to glory.

**—Terry Meeuwsen**
Co-host, *The 700 Club*
Former Miss America

Proverbs 3:6 says that God will direct our paths. God directed our paths to Cheryl and Harry Salem at the time our son, Jeremy, was diagnosed with second stage lymphoma cancer. At times, we walked in peace; other times, fear. The Salems exemplified steadfastness in the midst of their adversity with their daughter Gabrielle. Their lives of faith ministered peace and hope to our family in the midst of our storm.

**—John Shelby (and wife Trina)**
First Base Coach, L.A. Dodgers

We have long been blessed to know Harry and Cheryl Salem, both as our guests on television and as the closest of personal friends. We have witnessed firsthand how, out of their darkest tragedy, the Lord has birthed their greatest revelation. The understanding they set forth in *From Grief to Glory* stands upon a foundation of truth that we believe is crucial for all believers to embrace if we are to walk out our true destiny in Christ. We couldn't agree more with their declaration that Jesus came *"that He might destroy the works of the devil."*

Tragedy and loss aren't the result of a spiritual battle; rather they are opportunities for us to discover new treasures buried within His kingdom. They are opportunities to pursue the good fight of faith that declares that, no matter what comes our way, God is all-powerful at all times, working all things together for good for those who love Him and are called according to His purpose.

**—Matt and Laurie Crouch**
Gener8Xion Entertainment

Until pain becomes a gift, it can seem meaningless. The ability to move through grief and not get stuck in the process is at the heart of God's intention for His children. Do we grieve? Yes! Do we mourn? Yes! Do we stay there? No!

Over the past few years, Harry and Cheryl Salem have helped many to grow because of their transparency and authenticity in regard to the loss of their precious daughter. A great gift has come out of their pain. They have modeled a proven pathway to wholeness. Their willingness to share their experiences has made it possible for others to move from grief to glory. Thank you, Harry and Cheryl, for your continued willingness to be available to those who are yearning to process their pain, get past it, and see the gifts that lie beyond it.

**—Dr. Mark J. Chironna**
Overseer,
The Master's Touch International Church
Orlando, Florida

This book contains some of the most practical truths on moving from tragedy to triumph. This is not just theory, but the very relevant step-by-step experiences of a family that has been made more than whole after heartbreak. The Salems show us how to come out of the fire without even smelling like smoke.

**—Eastman and Angel Curtis**
Senior Pastors, Destiny Church
Broken Arrow, Oklahoma

Death has touched or will touch us all. *From Grief to Glory* allows you to walk in the footsteps of Cheryl and Harry Salem. For those who have ever lost a child or a loved one, this compelling, bold, yet compassionate book will help you to turn your sorrow into joy and your grief into glory.

**—Dwight and Zonelle Thompson**
Dwight Thompson World Outreach Ministries
Corona, California

This amazing book brings healing and deliverance from the agonizing spirit of grief and an unhealthy mourning process. Cheryl and Harry Salem are transparent, honest, and anointed as they walk you through their journey of brokenness and the power of God's healing.

**—Randy and Paula White**
Senior Pastors,
Without Walls International Church
Tampa, Florida

*From Grief to Glory* is a must-read for anyone who has lost a loved one. Harry and Cheryl Salem speak from firsthand experience after watching their little girl Gabrielle go home to be with the Lord. We highly recommend this book to all those in need of comfort.

**—Drs. Rodney and Adonica Howard-Browne**
Founders of Revival Ministries International,
Tampa, Florida

*From*

# GRIEF

*to*

# GLORY

REDISCOVERING LIFE AFTER LOSS

HARRY & CHERYL SALEM

WHITAKER
HOUSE

Unless otherwise indicated, all Scripture quotations are taken from the *New King James Version*, © 1979, 1980, 1982 by Thomas Nelson, Inc. Used by permission. All rights reserved. Scripture quotations marked (KJV) are from the King James Version of the Bible. Scripture quotations marked (NIV) are from the Holy Bible, *New International Version*, © 1973, 1978, 1984 by the International Bible Society. Used by permission. Scripture quotations marked (AMP) are taken from *The Amplified Bible, Old Testament*, © 1962, 1964, 1965, 1987 by the Zondervan Corporation, or from *The Amplified Bible, New Testament*, © 1954, 1958, 1987 by The Lockman Foundation. Used by permission.

Permission has been obtained from Harrison House to publish material from *From Mourning to Morning* (Harry and Cheryl Salem, Salem Family Ministries, Tulsa: Harrison House Publishers, © 2001).

Letter from George Herbert Walker Bush to his mother found on pages 9–10 used with permission from President George H. W. Bush.

**FROM GRIEF TO GLORY: REDISCOVERING LIFE AFTER LOSS**

ISBN: 0-88368-609-0
Printed in the United States of America
© 2003 by Salem Family Ministries

Salem Family Ministries
P.O. Box 701287
Tulsa, OK 74170
(918) 369-8008
e-mail: info@salemfamilyministries.org
website: www.salemfamilyministries.org

Whitaker House
30 Hunt Valley Circle
New Kensington, PA 15068
website: www.whitakerhouse.com

Library of Congress Cataloging-in-Publication Data

Salem, Harry.
  From grief to glory : rediscovering life after loss / Harry and Cheryl
Salem.
      p. cm.
   ISBN 0-88368-609-0 (alk. paper)
   1. Grief—Religious aspects—Christianity. 2. Children—Death—Religious
aspects—Christianity. 3. Bereavement—Religious aspects—Christianity. 4. Loss
(Psychology)—Religious aspects—Christianity. 5. Consolation. I.
Salem, Cheryl. II. Title.
   BV4907.S27 2003
   248.8'6—dc21                                              2003010893

No part of this book may be reproduced or transmitted in any form or by any means, electronic or mechanical, including photocopying, recording, or by any information storage and retrieval system, without permission in writing from the publisher.

    1 2 3 4 5 6 7 8 9 10 11 12 13 / 12 11 10 09 08 07 06 05 04 03

# "She Is Still with Us"
## by George Herbert Walker Bush

*We want to thank President George Herbert Walker Bush for passing along this wonderful excerpt from his own writings and giving us permission to add it to our book. Mr. President, you have blessed our family with your love, compassion, and strength. Thank you for being a part of our story!*

*—Harry and Cheryl Salem*

There is about our house a need. The running, pulsating restlessness of the four boys as they struggle to learn and grow...all this wonder needs a counter-part. We need some starched crisp frocks to go with all our torn-kneed blue jeans and helmets. We need some soft blond hair to offset those crew cuts. We need a doll house to stand firm against our forts and rackets and thousand baseball cards. We need a cut-out star to play alone while the others battle....

We need a legitimate Christmas angel—one who doesn't have cuffs beneath the dress.

We need someone who's afraid of frogs.

We need someone to cry when I get mad—not argue.

We need a little one who can kiss without leaving egg or jam or gum.

We need a girl.

We had one once—she'd fight and cry and play and make her way just like the rest. But there was about her a certain softness.

She was patient—her hugs were just a little less wiggly.

Like them, she'd climb in to sleep with me, but somehow she'd fit.

She didn't boot and flip and wake me up with pug nose and mischievous eyes a challenging quarter-inch from my sleeping face.

No—she'd stand beside our bed till I felt her there. Silently and comfortable, she'd put those precious, fragrant locks against my chest and fall asleep.

Her peace made me feel strong, and so very important.

"My Daddy" had a caress, a certain ownership which touched a slightly different spot than the "Hi Dad" I love so much.

But she is still with us. We need her and yet we have her. We can't touch her, and yet we can feel her.

We hope she'll stay in our house for a long, long time.

**—President George Herbert Walker Bush**
From a letter to his mother, most likely written in 1958, in regard to his feelings concerning the loss of his daughter, Robin, who died of leukemia at the age of three in 1953.

# Dedication

We dedicate this book to the most precious gifts that God has allowed us to keep with us here on earth, our sons Harry III and Roman. You have stood with us, prayed over us, and encouraged us more than anyone else. While you were grieving for your sister, you both exhibited the most precious spirits of concern for us. You never focused on yourselves, only on our family being restored. God has seen your hearts and your actions, and He alone knows just how much you have hurt without ever complaining about it. You have helped us find our joy, our recovery, and our restoration. God sent it to our family from heaven, and you were the messengers who carried it to us. You two are more than precious; you are irreplaceable! You are anointed young men of God, called for such a time as this, and you have answered the call. Thank you for being our sons. We love you more than words can say. We are so proud of you both, not just for today, but for eternity!

# Acknowledgments

There are not enough words to say how much we appreciate our precious friend and cowriter, Vicki Case. You have taken our tear-stained words, thoughts, and prayers, and have helped us make them relevant and understandable to all those who will read these pages. Thank you for your months of dedication, writing, and praying in helping us give birth to this heartfelt act of love for God's people.

We pray that this book will be a vital part of the restoration process to all who read it. It has been a labor of love for us, not only because of the hours we spent searching our own hearts, but also because of the countless memories we sifted through to put this book into words. We believe that the eternal rewards of this book will be heard, seen, and felt like gentle waves of mercy throughout God's precious people. We love you eternally!

# Contents

# Introduction:

## "Beauty for Ashes"

### By Harry and Cheryl

*To console those who mourn in Zion, to give them beauty for ashes, the oil of joy for mourning, the garment of praise for the spirit of heaviness; that they may be called trees of righteousness, the planting of the LORD, that He may be glorified.*
—Isaiah 61:3

It has been a little more than three years since our beloved six-year-old daughter Gabrielle went home to be with the Lord. She took the trip we will all take someday; she just took it a little earlier than we did. Now, she is waiting for the rest of her family to catch up to her in glory. That knowledge helps us keep in mind that she is in our future, not our past. But even with the sweet assurance of joining her again in heaven

someday, we still must live in the here and now. Since the time Gabrielle went on to the Lord, much has happened in our lives. There has been pain, sorrow, confusion, and heartache. Many, many tears have been shed and sometimes still are shed. But, most importantly, God has increased our understanding of Him and His plan for our lives, and, today, we look back and see things more clearly from His perspective rather than just our own.

Right after Gabrielle left to be with the Lord, we struggled mightily in our flesh, fighting against nearly unbearable pain and anguish. A precious part of our lives had been taken from us, and we didn't understand why. We didn't want to understand, either. It was just too much to think about in that time of intense grief. Still, questions arose in our minds: Why did our daughter have to leave us? Why did she have to suffer so much? Why did God let this happen to our family? If these questions weren't enough to weigh us down mentally and emotionally, we found that we also had to answer countless questions from people around us who had watched us during our daughter's fight for life. They, too, had questions—questions about our faith, our ministry, and our futures. What's more, many other people we had ministered to through the years came to us and asked us to help them with *their* pain in the midst of our own anguish. In those first few days after Gabrielle went home, when our spirits still felt wounded and tender, it seemed beyond our ability to bear our own incredible pain and the pain that others were going through. How could we possibly minister healing to others when we ourselves desperately needed healing and restoration in our own lives? This was the one question that, at times, weighed the most heavily on our minds.

So we prayed.

We prayed that God would not only help us live through the pain we felt each day but also give us answers to our grief that would help others facing the same kind of pain. If God was going to bless us with healing and restoration, we wanted to be able to turn around and bless others with what He taught us. Somehow, we knew, God could take the agony we felt and use it for good. (See Romans 8:28.) After all, He had done that very thing when His Son Jesus died on the cross. At that moment, the devil surely must have thought he had won a major battle, if not the war, against God. But God knew better. Jesus was resurrected, and He lives on forevermore as the Lord and Savior of the world! Even when His ministry seemed to come to a bleak

*What the devil means for evil, God will use for good.*

end on the hill of Calvary, it was really just the beginning—for you and for us and for the rest of the world. Satan can't see past the moment; he has no ability to know the future as God does. That's why he tries to get us to focus on the moment, especially when we are overwhelmed by intensely painful emotions like grief and sorrow.

After our daughter went home to heaven, we had some very painful moments when it seemed like nothing would ever work out for good in our lives. Satan tried to destroy our family and our family's ministry, but he didn't—and he never will. God is at the root of our lives, and we leaned on Him and looked to Him for answers in the midst of the grieving process. We knew that what

the devil meant for evil, God would use for good. (See Genesis 50:20.) We knew that weeping would endure for a night—for a season—but we also knew that joy would come in the morning. (See Psalm 30:5.) Praise God that we have endured the process and are living the promise!

Today, our family is ministering to more people than ever before because God has been faithful in upholding and strengthening us as we stand in faith on His Word. We are seeing how God has turned evil into good as we are now able to minister to countless people who are stricken with sorrow because of a departed loved one.

*Life is about overcoming.*

This new door of ministry has been opened to us, and we are making the most of it by teaching others what God has taught us. Because we have been through the fires of affliction, we are able to stand next to these people and give them a shoulder to cry on. More than that, we do, at times, feel to some degree what they are feeling. We still fight the war of the mind against the negative and condemning thoughts that come to us from time to time. But God uses even that for good. We have come to find that people's lives are touched deeply when they hear from men, women, and even children of faith who have overcome and are overcoming adversity in their own lives.

Life is about overcoming for each one of us, no matter what tragedy or trial has befallen us. It is never about our troubles or problems; it is about how we face them and overcome them. It is so easy to think that, because we have trials, we have stepped out of God's

blessing in our lives. But we have found just the opposite to be true. It is the trials and tribulations of life
that allow us to see how God works in our lives and
blesses us. We may not understand why God allows
certain things into our lives, and we may never understand why God does what He does because, as He says,
*"For as the heavens are higher than the earth, so are My
ways higher than your ways, and My thoughts than your
thoughts"* (Isaiah 55:9). However, no matter how much
pain, heartache, or anguish enters our lives, we can still
be given *"beauty for ashes"* (Isaiah 61:3)—we can still
come through the fires of grief and mourning with a
song of praise and celebration to our Lord Jesus Christ.

It is for this reason that we are writing this book. We
long to help those who are trying to draw some meaning, understanding, and comfort from the departure of a
loved one. With this book, we hope to motivate people
to move through their grief and get back into life. God
has increased the depth of our knowledge and experience of Him through our time of grief and mourning,
and we want to share what we have learned. We know
the questions and concerns that arise after the passing
of a loved one, and we understand the feelings that
sometimes rage within us during the grieving process.
We know very well that it sometimes seems as if life may
never be worth living again. But we know even better
that life is always worth living in the Lord!

A journey through grief is something we will all
probably experience at some point in our lives. If you are
on that journey right now, we pray that this book will
help you find peace and joy as you move from pain and
anguish to restoration, recovery, and healing. No longer
do you need to let grief and heartache rule your house.

Instead, by faith, you can move from grief to glory and enjoy the promise of a new day in the grace and mercy of God! *"Through the LORD's mercies we are not consumed, because His compassions fail not. They are new every morning; great is Your faithfulness"* (Lamentations 3:22–23).

## Chapter One
# *Blindsided:*

# *Standing Strong*
# *When Tragedy Strikes*

### *By Harry*

More often than not, tragedy and adversity hit us without warning, like a violent, unexpected storm that leaves a person reeling from the sudden impact. Here in Oklahoma, it seems as though the weather can change in an instant. One minute, the summer sun is shining brightly, and a warm breeze is blowing. Then, only a short time later, the sky is dark, and huge drops of cold rain are crashing to the ground. Sometimes, the dark clouds overhead begin to droop downward, and, soon enough, a funnel-shaped cloud mass descends toward the earth. The tornado that follows can bring incredible devastation where, just moments before, a peaceful serenity

existed and people happily went about their business on a pleasant summer day. This is how we felt when our family was blindsided by adversity on January 11, 1999.

We were a happy, healthy, as-normal-as-can-be American family. Along with Cheryl and me, there were our two boys—Harry, twelve, and Roman, a few days shy of his ninth birthday—and then there was Gabrielle, our precious little five-year-old daughter. As a family, we couldn't have been more content in life. We were busy doing the work of the Lord together, ministering across the country, and we felt a great sense of fulfillment. Countless lives were being changed through our ministry, and we were grateful to God for the opportunities He had given us. As a husband and father, I was proud of my family and what we were accomplishing together for the Lord. In fact, during 1998, we had one of the most wonderful years of our lives together while ministering as a family. All five of us traveled together throughout the United States and Canada, ministering in more than 250 services along the way. We were sure that 1999 would hold even greater things for us, both as a family and a ministry.

At the start of 1999, we returned from an incredible New Year's ministry trip. We had seen God accomplish marvelous things, and, on the ride home, we were having the most fun-filled and joyous time ever as a family. At one point, Cheryl even commented, "Life can't get any better than this!"

Little did we suspect the turn our lives would soon take.

# Whose Report Will You Believe?

About a week after we arrived home in Tulsa, Oklahoma, we noticed that Gabrielle would slowly turn her head to follow our conversations or to look at something as it went by her. At first, we weren't alarmed because we knew she couldn't hear out of her left ear. Often, when she wanted to hear us better, she would turn her head in our direction. Sometimes, she would even move my chin so that I aimed my voice directly at her. However, we quickly began to realize that, this time, something was different. Gabrielle was turning her head not to hear better but to see. She was unable to follow Cheryl's finger with her eyes as it moved back and forth in front of her. At that point, we knew something was wrong, and we knew we had to get our daughter to the doctor as soon as we could.

We phoned our family doctor and told him everything we could about Gabrielle's behavior. He recommended that we take Gabrielle to an ophthalmologist, which we did immediately. After examining our daughter, the ophthalmologist asked me to step into the hall with him. He said that Gabrielle's inability to track movement with her eyes was a condition known as "doll's eyes." The cause, he said, was usually some sort of pressure on the brain. Beyond that, he said he couldn't give us any definitive diagnosis, but he quickly ordered an MRI and called a specialist.

Later that same afternoon, Cheryl and I took Gabrielle to the hospital for the MRI test. When it was completed, the medical technician who performed the test saw the distress we were both in and took me aside. While he wasn't permitted to give us the specific

diagnosis, he told me that something was in Gabrielle's brain stem, and "It's not good." I told Cheryl, and, like me, she was crushed. Yet, we remained hopeful that we might get a better report the next morning when we were to go over the test results with a radiologist.

Our hopes were quickly dashed early the next day at the hospital as the radiologist gave us the grim report: "It is a malignant tumor, known as a glioma, in the brain stem, and it is inoperable. It is one of the most aggressive types of tumors. Your daughter has two months, maybe six, to live."

*God still performs miracles.*

Cheryl and I felt like the wind had been knocked out of us. Our minds were screaming, "No, this can't be! Not our little girl!" However, we would not allow such thoughts to rule our minds. We immediately went into battle mode spiritually. We had been given a negative report, a report that said our precious daughter was not going to be with us much longer. We knew, though, that God still performs miracles, and we chose to believe that our daughter would be healed.

We had been through so much already in our lives, and we knew that nothing was too difficult for God. (See Jeremiah 32:27.) We had lost a son to a miscarriage. Then, when Cheryl was pregnant with Gabrielle, she hemorrhaged so badly that the doctors believed she had lost the baby. We refused to believe that negative report, and, after seven months of bed rest, Cheryl gave birth to our daughter. Then, not long after Gabrielle's birth, Cheryl battled through an eighteen-month bout

of depression. We had known in each of those difficult circumstances that God was in control, and we still knew after receiving the tragic report about Gabrielle that God was in control and more than able to handle this latest challenge to our faith in Him. (See Ephesians 3:20–21.)

We left the hospital that day and drove directly to Richard and Lindsay Roberts' home (Lindsay is my sister). Richard called his father and mother, Oral and Evelyn, and, with them on the phone, we all prayed together over our daughter. We knew we would not be able to endure the long road ahead of us without the help and support of those closest to us. We also knew that, somehow, our lives had to go on in spite of the tragedy that had struck our family. That night, we decided to go ahead with an already planned appearance on the television show, *The Hour of Healing.* Even though we felt the incredible weight of the evil report we had received, we knew in our spirits that God wanted us to stand in faith upon His promises and that we could minister to others even as they themselves ministered to us.

## *The Long Journey Begins*

As soon as we returned home from the Roberts' house, we called everyone we could think of to stand with us in prayer for Gabrielle. We also did all we could in the natural for our daughter. Her medical reports were sent to St. Jude's Hospital in Memphis, Tennessee. One of the specialists there requested another MRI scan, which we had done immediately. After examining the reports and the new scan, the specialist at St. Jude's called us, confirmed the diagnosis, and said, "I'm

sorry. There is nothing we can do." Then, he hung up abruptly.

Undaunted, we soon got in touch with one of the top neurosurgeons at Mt. Sinai Hospital in New York City. We had learned of his reputation as one of the few surgeons in the world who could operate on a tumor in the brain stem. He looked over all of Gabrielle's reports and scans, and he quickly set up a conference call with two other specialists in New York. After meeting on the phone with these specialists, he contacted us and delivered yet another blow: There wasn't anything he could do or recommend to save our little girl.

By this time, we had become open to anything that might help Gabrielle. Another option presented itself in the form of a physician in Houston, Texas, who used an experimental treatment methodology on brain tumors. Using this alternative form of medicine, the physician had successfully treated many brain tumor patients who had not been helped by traditional methods. After much discussion and prayer, Cheryl and I decided that the Lord wanted us to pursue this form of treatment for Gabrielle.

This alternative treatment would not be easy—for Gabrielle or the rest of the family. For nearly a month, we all stayed in Houston and learned about the treatment process. The first step was to have a catheter port inserted into Gabrielle's chest to receive intravenous medications and to facilitate blood drawings. From then on, our daughter had to carry a fifteen-pound portable IV pump in a backpack wherever she went, day or night. Cheryl, along with Tracey, a family friend who was more like a sister to us, learned the treatment process by sitting

through hours of instruction on how to prepare and administer IV solutions, how to care for the catheter port, how to draw blood, and how to record all vital information on a daily basis. I would stay with Gabrielle when Cheryl was being trained, and I took her to her daily doctor's visits. Thankfully, my mom was there to stay with our sons. That month flew by and seemed like a perpetual whirlwind of activity. I recall not changing my clothes for an entire week at one point. Always on the go and always under enormous emotional strain, I would barely eat and ended up losing thirty-five pounds that month.

In an attempt to keep business as usual for the whole family, we did not let our sons know the severity of Gabrielle's illness, and we continued to travel and minister as a family. This was ultimately my decision. I didn't want us to focus on the negative and keep ourselves from living life or doing what God called us to do. So, we loaded all the necessary medical equipment into our motor coach, which became more of a traveling hospital than anything else, and set out on the road again. We eventually settled into a routine for each stop we made. When we reached our destination, we would check into the hotel, and Tracey would first go into the rooms to clean and arrange them while Cheryl got Gabrielle ready. The boys and I would carry all the medical equipment and supplies into the rooms and set it up. Finally, I would carry Gabrielle from the motor coach and place her in a chair I had rigged with wheels just for her, to make it easier to transport her from one place to another. By the time we were all settled into our rooms, we were completely drained.

The daily routine was an incredible drain as well. Tracey prepared the IV bags, and Cheryl did the

hands-on care of Gabrielle—administering medications, flushing the catheter port, and drawing blood samples. It was up to me to find a lab or hospital wherever we were so I could drop off the blood samples for testing three times a week. Our diets changed, as well, because of Gabrielle's treatment plan. She ate only organic and natural foods, as she had to avoid all salts or sugars, so we did, too.

Our sons also did all they could for Gabrielle, playing with her for hours on end and enduring the blandest of foods because they knew it was what Gabrielle had to eat. Not once did either of them complain. It didn't matter if it meant cleaning up the bathroom, getting up in the wee hours of the morning for Gabrielle's next blood draw, or being awakened in the middle of the night because their little sister was violently throwing up. They would often make her breakfast in the morning, fashioning a smiley face out of eggs and toast. They also helped entertain her, watching the same movies with her over and over again or allowing her to soak them with her giant water gun. At one point, young Harry and Roman received a financial gift they had received for speaking at a church and then used it to buy Gabrielle a handheld video game system. To our boys, Gabrielle wasn't a cancer patient who was slowly dying. She was their precious sister whom they loved. With that kind of love in their hearts, they pitched right in and did what they could to make their sister's life more bearable and enjoyable.

## *Home in Heaven*

Gabrielle fought the disease in her body with every fiber of her being and her spirit, too. She wouldn't let the

disease beat her, which meant she wasn't going to stop singing and ministering to others on our trips. During her eleven-month fight against the cancer in her body, she ministered in more than a hundred churches across the country. She simply would not let some disease stop her from operating in the anointing on her life as a minister of the Gospel. At one point, while we were in Houston at the clinic, we met up with Oral Roberts, who was there to pray for Pastor John Osteen. We asked Oral if he would pray for Gabrielle while he was there. Oral agreed, but, when he told Gabrielle he wanted to pray for her, she insisted that *she* wanted to pray for *him*. Afterward, Oral said he felt more anointing flowing from Gabrielle than any other child he had known. In Oral's words, Gabrielle was "unstoppable." But the disease finally took its toll on her tiny body. The steroids she was on ballooned her five-year-old frame from thirty-seven pounds to ninety-seven pounds. Slowly, but surely, the days turned into months. Gabrielle's sixth birthday came and went, and her condition continued to deteriorate.

Each night, Cheryl and I would take turns sitting up with Gabrielle. By November 1999, we knew the end was near. One night that month, Cheryl had sat up with her throughout the night. The next morning at 6:55, I went into the room, and Cheryl said, "I'm so sleepy. I have to lay my head down for just five minutes." Cheryl immediately fell into a deep sleep, and I took over watching Gabrielle, who soon opened her eyes and started blowing kisses. I didn't know if they were for me, or if she saw Jesus in heaven and was showing Him how much she loved Him. A few minutes later, at 7:05 A.M. on November 23, 1999, Gabrielle Christian Salem joined Jesus in heaven. Just before she breathed her last breath on earth, she was still blowing kisses. Whether the kisses

were for me or for Jesus, our little girl left this world and entered heaven doing what she did best during her time with us: showing her love for others.

## *Where the Battle Is Truly Fought*

From the very beginning of our fight for our daughter's life, we experienced an incredible range of emotions. One moment, we were enraged that such a thing could be happening to our daughter. The next moment, we cried until it seemed we had no tears left. We would stand in faith and feel strong in the Lord, then come under yet another attack from the enemy. Satan tried to weaken us through assaults we knew would come— pain, heartache, anger, frustration, and the like. But he also hit us with things we would have never expected, such as callous treatment from some of those around us and being turned down when we were desperate for someone's help. People sometimes judged us because our daughter had gone to heaven. These people treated us as if we had given her the cancer that afflicted her or as though we didn't have enough faith in God to heal her. Back and forth our emotions went, and, sometimes, it seemed like we went with them. We didn't ask for this difficult and ultimately tragic event in our lives, but we knew it wasn't up to us. We wanted to experience healing and restoration, but we often resisted the process of grief that would bring us victory. Still, after Gabrielle went home, we knew that if we were to move from grief to glory, we would have to go through the process, through whatever we faced day by day.

Once, during His ministry on earth, Jesus told a distressed man, *"Do not be afraid; only believe"* (Mark

5:36). The real test of our faith is whether we will *"only believe"* when what we feel inside tells us to give up all hope. Why should we believe? Jesus said, *"In the world you will have tribulation; but be of good cheer, I have overcome the world"* (John 16:33). We need to remind ourselves that Jesus is greater than our circumstances or anything that the devil might throw at us. (See 1 John 4:4.) When we finally determine in our hearts that we *are* going to believe and stand strong in our faith in God, then we can be assured that we will have victory over our circumstances, no matter how bad they appear to be. *"For whatever is born of God overcomes the world. And this is the victory that has overcome the world; our faith"* (1 John 5:4).

The key to overcoming is simple, yet completely impossible without the help of the Lord. To *"fight the good fight of faith"* (1 Timothy 6:12), we need to know what we will do if tragedy strikes. In other words, we need to be prepared for battle.

> *We need to be prepared for battle.*

As I mentioned earlier, tragedy rarely gives us any warning before it strikes. It comes out of the blue and blindsides us. That means we need to prepare now and stay prepared. It means we need to do the "little" things every day—read and study the Bible, meditate on God's Word, praise and worship the Lord, spend time fellowshipping with other believers. The basics of the Christian life not only deepen our knowledge of and affection for God, but they also help us *"stand"* after we have *"done all"* (Ephesians 6:13) and to *"fight the good fight of faith."*

Remember, the Bible says to *"resist the devil"* (James 4:7), not to fight against him. Why? Because he is already a defeated foe! Jesus defeated him for all eternity when He died on the cross and victoriously rose again on the third day. Jesus' defeat of Satan means that the devil is not directly part of our fight of faith. After all, why would we need to contend with a beaten enemy? Even the archangel Michael didn't attempt to fight with Satan one-on-one. Instead, he declared to the devil, *"The Lord rebuke you!"* (Jude 9).

So, if Satan is not our main opponent, then what is it we fight when we attempt to stand strong in faith? We fight a war of the mind, a place where we find *"imaginations"* and *"every high thing"* that comes against our faith in God (2 Corinthians 10:5 KJV). It takes spiritual strength to wage war against the thoughts and emotions that assail our minds. It takes spiritual preparation to be *"transformed by the renewing of your mind"* (Romans 12:2). That's why we need to keep strengthening and deepening our relationships with God when it seems like everything in life is going smoothly. The day-to-day habits that bring us closer to the Lord are what will determine our ability to fight a good fight of faith when times of adversity come. We often get too short-sighted, thinking that, if everything in our lives is going well, we can rest easy in our spiritual walks. We too easily fall into being earthly minded instead of eternally minded. (See Colossians 3:1–2.)

We quickly find out what is in our hearts and minds when adversity or tragedy comes into our lives. If we've been growing in our relationships with God, our faith will manifest itself in our words and actions in times of trouble. However, if we've been slack in our daily

walks with the Lord, then we are going to find ourselves between a rock and a hard place when tragedy occurs and the fight of faith takes center stage in our lives. The sad thing is that, when you feel like you're drowning in life, there is no time to take swimming lessons. It's too late. You either know how to swim, or it's over. We need to remember this so that our faith in God won't be found wanting when trials come our way. Too many Christians make the mistake of living their lives spiritually unprepared. This is tan-tamount to a soldier going to war without any preparation. The time to learn about warfare is *before* the bullets start flying. No soldier goes to class to find out how to fight when there is an actual battle raging all around him.

*Our faith will manifest itself in our words and actions.*

It's the same for us as Christians. We need to be growing in our Christian maturity by going deeper into the things of God on a daily basis. We need to get God's Word into our spirits, into our hearts, and into our minds if we ever want to be able to stand in faith on His promises when adversity arises in our lives. Just like soldiers, we as Christians need to train ourselves for future battles. (See Psalm 144:1.) We need to dress ourselves in the spiritual armor of God that will protect us and allow us to take back what the enemy tries to steal from us. (See Ephesians 6:11–17.) Our minds must be firmly grounded in the truth of God that declares *"we are more than conquerors through Him who loved us"* (Romans 8:37). But all this must be done *before* we are forced to walk through the fires of affliction. As Cheryl likes to say, "Prior preparation prevents poor per-formance."

Do you want to know the simplest and most basic key to overcoming tragedy when it strikes? Preparation. Preparation is the key to victory. Preparation will bring us closer to Jesus, and, when life takes a turn for the worse, it will remind us that the Lord is there for us when tragedy blindsides us. Remember that nothing surprises God Almighty. It is He who is able to bring us through the fire so that there is not even a hint of "smoke" about us. (See Daniel 3:27.) We cannot overcome unexpected adversity in our own strength, but, by being prepared to *"fight the good fight of faith"* (1 Timothy 6:12), we can confidently declare, *"I can do all things through Christ who strengthens me"* (Philippians 4:13)!

## *Points to Ponder*

1.  a. When you face tough times in your life, do you feel prepared to deal with them? Why, or why not?

    b. What are some things you could be doing (or doing more often) to better prepare yourself for the trials of life?

2.  If you are currently dealing with a tragedy or in the midst of an intense struggle in your life, what are three things you can do at this moment to help you *"fight the good fight of faith"* (1 Timothy 6:12)?

    •

    •

    •

## Chapter Two

# Homecoming:

# Taking the First Steps Back toward Life

### By Cheryl

For eleven months, our entire family held on in faith that God would heal Gabrielle. Then, on that early morning in late November, Gabrielle went home to be with the Lord. God made the decision to bring her close to Him, and who wouldn't want our little blue-eyed, blonde bundle of joy nearby? We didn't know—and still don't—why she was the first one of our immediate family to go home, but we trusted that God could bring good out of what the devil meant for evil.

Still, as a mother, I was heartbroken. What had happened? Why did it have to happen? After all, we had believed for the best. We had stood in faith. We hadn't

wavered or doubted. Every day, we fought *"the good fight of faith"* (1 Timothy 6:12) against the negative and depressing thoughts that assailed our minds. We confessed God's good promises and firmly believed that He would heal her here on earth. But our daughter still left us and went to heaven.

Gabrielle's home-going didn't signal the end of our fight of faith; rather, it ushered in a new battle to remain *"strong in the Lord and in the power of His might"* (Ephesians 6:10). The emotions that immediately followed Gabrielle's departure to heaven seemed unbearable. The pain and anguish were beyond torture at times, but we still took a giant step forward and declared by faith, "Lord, we trust You!" However, just because we declared our intention to trust God, we weren't immune to the pain and anguish that came. Depressing, condemning thoughts came. Thoughts of who to blame arose in my mind. I so badly wanted to blame someone for what happened, and I always put myself at the top of the list. I just didn't understand how the devil could do this to us.

It was then that the Holy Spirit gently said to me, "Do you think that the devil can ever 'slip one past' the Father?"

I knew immediately that the Spirit was confirming to me that Satan cannot do anything without the Father's knowledge. As hard as it was for me to acknowledge and accept that God allowed this tragedy to happen, I had such a peace and sense of relief knowing that the devil cannot ever defeat our God. Satan is not God, and he cannot win—ever! The devil is a defeated foe, and we need to get this fact into our hearts and minds for the battles of faith we will inevitably face.

In spite of the fact that I felt like my heart had been torn out, I remained confident in the fact that God was still in control of our lives and that His healing power would sustain us. With that in mind, Harry and I knew the first thing we had to do—for us and for the boys—was to get out of our house for a time. We didn't want our home to become a house of bondage, a four-walled prison for our minds with no way out of the halls of countless memories of our daughter.

Thankfully, friends of ours on the West Coast invited us to visit. Benny and Suzanne Hinn asked us to do a television show with them, and Matt and Lori Crouch wanted us to join them on TBN. So, we packed up and headed west. I just knew in my heart that we needed to get right back into ministering to others. It was our calling—our assignment from God. In addition, by ministering to others, we would also be ministering to ourselves, I believed. It was a reason to go on—a purpose in a time of confusion and

*We needed to get right back into ministering to others.*

pain. Even though we didn't always feel like ministering to others and even though we thought it was too much to bear at times, we moved on in faith. We kept meditating on God's goodness and grace despite the fact that, at times, we didn't feel like there was much good about life anymore.

We pressed on, knowing that our journey through adversity offered us an opportunity to positively affect the lives of others for the Lord. We knew it was easy to sing praises to God in the best of times and forget Him when things got tough. What made an impact in

people's lives was seeing others still praising and thanking God while they went through the fire. That is the testimony we wanted to have and to share wherever we went.

# The Hard Road Home

Getting away for a while helped our family immensely, but it became difficult for all of us when it came time to go back home. The very thought of going back to our house was too much to bear. Christmas was fast approaching when we packed up and started back to Tulsa after our time on the West Coast. There seemed to be little joy for us during this season of celebration, especially because of what Christmas meant to our family in the past. Christmas was always the high point of our family's year. We would celebrate it for more than a month. The tree and all the lights would go up on Thanksgiving Day so that we could begin the season on a day of thanks as we looked forward to the celebration of Christ's birth.

Celebrating Christmas was a complete family affair for us. The children would help put up the lights outside, and, even though our lights weren't the straightest in the neighborhood, we still loved looking at them because we had done it together. Inside the house, we always had two trees. One was in the family room, and it was decorated by the kids with handmade ornaments that they had crafted in school. The other tree was what the boys called "Mom's fancy tree." Each year, I would decorate it with angel ornaments, and then, to finish it, we would lift up Gabrielle—our little angel—and let her put an angel ornament on the treetop.

Christmas was such a happy, special time for our family. It gave us such a sense of family fulfillment. But this season, there would be none of that.

As we drove home from the Tulsa airport in late December, our raw, wounded emotions were running high and beginning to rise to the surface. My heart ached so badly for Roman and young Harry. It was Christmas, a special time for children, and they would have no chance to celebrate the sweet peace and joy of the season.

At one point during the drive, Roman piped up, "We don't even have a Christmas tree."

"We didn't put up the Christmas lights like we always do," Harry solemnly added. "We haven't bought any presents."

Both of them had tears in their eyes, and I could tell that their hearts were hurting just as much as mine. We felt so cheated right then, as if our family had been plundered, robbed, and destroyed. (See Isaiah 42:22.) Our battle-weary spirits had reached rock bottom, and, now, we had to drive home to a house that would be easy to find on our street—it would be the dark one, the one without any cheerful lights. Inside, there would be no trees, no decorations that showed how much we loved Christmas and what it stood for. Even if we went out and hurriedly bought a tree, how would we ever be able to put the angel on the top?

As we turned the corner to our house, our hearts were broken, and a spirit of heaviness permeated the car. Then, we saw our house, and we quickly felt the spirit of heaviness begin to lift, replaced now by the

garment of praise. (See Isaiah 61:3.) Our house was adorned with the most beautiful Christmas lights we had ever seen! There were even lights on the roof (something we hadn't bothered with since Harry fell while putting them up one Christmas). We basked in the twinkling of the sparkling lights as we made our way to the front door. Once inside the house, we saw an even more incredible scene. The interior of our house looked like something out of a Norman Rockwell painting. Decorations were everywhere, and Christmas warmth just radiated from the walls of our home. In the living room, we even found a Christmas tree topped with a beautiful angel.

How our hearts rejoiced! The love we felt at that moment cannot be expressed. Our family and friends who had stood by us through it all hadn't stopped doing so when Gabrielle went home to heaven. They kept showing us their love and the love of Christ by reaching out to us with this beautiful and heartfelt gesture. Little did they know that this simple act of love and kindness would be a new beginning for our family. God used these precious people to start the rebirth of our family—the trading of ashes for beauty. At that moment, as we stood in the glow of our graciously decorated home, we as a family declared a rekindling of our lives and spirits, and even more, a rekindling of the lives and spirits of all God's children from that day forward!

## Don't Listen to the Devil!

Satan tried to paint the bleakest picture possible for us as we drove through Tulsa on our way home that evening. He wanted us to dwell on everything that would

be missing from our lives that Christmas. He desired for us to wallow in our own self-pity and miss out on the joy of celebrating the birth of our Lord and Savior Jesus Christ. Thankfully, God was there, working on our behalf to turn a potentially devastating homecoming into a beacon of light for our lives.

The devil will always try to paint the worst picture possible for God's children, but we must refuse to look at our circumstances. Satan will tell those of us who have said goodbye to loved ones that we will have to live in pain every day for the rest of our lives—that we can never truly be happy again and that God will never be able to restore us to joy. He'll make sure we understand that we will never see our loved ones again on earth and that, every time we think of them, we will feel hollow and painfully empty. These attacking thoughts are the very things that will truly keep us in bondage—if we let them. It's up to us, because, just as Satan paints a picture for us, so

*God's picture is one of healing, restoration, and recovery.*

does God. God's picture is one of healing, restoration, and recovery. It's one of love, joy, and peace. God doesn't condemn us to a life sentence of pain, guilt, and condemnation. That kind of thinking only comes from one place—Satan himself. We need to recognize the accuser who brings these thoughts to our minds and refuse to receive his little "gifts."

Do you think our loved ones in heaven would approve of us accepting Satan's way of looking at our lives? I'll bet if we were able to talk to them, they would shake their heads and tell us that they want us to

remember why they were so special to us. They would remind us that faith in God is a lifelong commitment that isn't always easy. They would tell us that God is the giver of restoration and that Satan is the master of destruction.

Our loved ones who are now awaiting us in heaven have a perspective that we cannot enjoy with our natural eyes. They are able to understand things from an eternal perspective. We may not be able to "see" in hindsight why things happened as they did, but we can still become more eternally minded by setting our minds *"on things above, not on things on the earth"* (Colossians 3:2). Satan seeks to get our thoughts on earthly matters that will cause us greater pain and anguish than we are already suffering. His attacks are meant to confuse us and to keep our minds occupied with something other than the incredible promises of God.

*The God who made the universe knows us and cares about us!*

Thankfully, we know that *"God is not the author of confusion but of peace"* (1 Corinthians 14:33). We know that Jesus is our *"Prince of Peace"* (Isaiah 9:6) and that He told us, *"Peace I leave with you, My peace I give to you; not as the world gives do I give to you. Let not your heart be troubled, neither let it be afraid"* (John 14:27). When we remind ourselves of this great peace that we can experience in Christ, then *"the peace of God, which surpasses all understanding, will guard [our] hearts and minds through Christ Jesus"* (Philippians 4:7).

Consider also that God knows us better than anyone else, and He wants us to recover from tragedy and enjoy

the dawn of a new morning in our lives. Think about that! The God who made the universe knows us and cares about us!

*For You formed my inward parts; You covered me in my mother's womb. I will praise You, for I am fearfully and wonderfully made; marvelous are Your works, and that my soul knows very well. My frame was not hidden from You, when I was made in secret, and skillfully wrought in the lowest parts of the earth. Your eyes saw my substance, being yet unformed. And in Your book they all were written, the days fashioned for me, when as yet there were none of them. How precious also are Your thoughts to me, O God! How great is the sum of them! If I should count them, they would be more in number than the sand; when I awake, I am still with You.*
(Psalm 139:13–18)

God, through the Holy Spirit, speaks to us through our spirits. (See John 14:26.) He touches our innermost being when He wants to whisper thoughts of love and peace to us. Satan, on the other hand, focuses his energy on directing our attention to what we can see and feel. He tries to get us to stay earthly minded by keeping us preoccupied with temporal things—our thoughts and feelings. We need to remember that our thoughts and feelings are completely subject to change. They are not eternal; they will come to an end. That's why we must believe more in what we *cannot* see than what we can see. That's the life of faith in God. Faith says to us during our thoughts and feelings of loss that God is a good God who will bring beauty to our lives

*45*

once more. This is where our strength and hope must come from, not the false, negative things we see or feel.

## Become Someone Else's Miracle

If we keep our eyes of faith on God and His promises of restoration and recovery, He will never allow us to go through adversity without molding us into more valuable vessels of His love and grace. If we let Him have His way with us, He will work through our lives and bring miracles to those who are desperate for a touch from God. We can expect miracles to follow the storms of our lives. We can find a place where we can minister to others in ways we would have never dreamed of. And why not? If we stay strong in the Lord during times of tragedy and adversity, we will be changed people. We won't be the same as when the trial came into our lives. We'll be stronger and wiser, and we will have more to give to others who are in need.

Just think: Satan was trying to make us weaker, but, in reality, all he did was bring us to a place of greater strength and faith. How could this be? Simple: We endured the process with the promise of God always in our sights. Did we always feel like doing it? No. Did we always think in our minds that things were going to work out for the best? Of course not. But, in our spirits, we remained immovable. Remember that we are to live by faith, not by what we see or feel! (See 2 Corinthians 5:7.) When we remain steadfast in our faith in God, we will come forth from the trials of life *"as gold"* (Job 23:10)—reflecting the pure light of Christ's love to others who may be yearning for a miracle in their own lives.

It's faith that allows us to become someone else's miracle in life. Do you think our friends and family felt like spending an incredible amount of time decorating our house for us? Probably not. My guess is that they probably had so much going on with their own families that they really didn't have the time to bless us like they did. But they did it anyway. They became our miracles because they acted out of faithful and loving hearts.

We all need miracles at certain times in our lives. These miracles may be the simplest of things. Maybe it's hearing a word of encouragement. People everywhere are starving to hear words such as, "Good job! Keep up the good work." Or, "Did you know that you've really made an impact in my life?" And, "Hey, I know you've had it rough, but I want you to know that I'm praying for you."

The author of Hebrews exhorted us to look after the needs of those around us by saying, *"Let us encourage one another"* (Hebrews 10:25 NIV). In his letter to the Christians in Rome, the apostle Paul said, *"Let us pursue the things which make for peace and the things by which one may edify another"* (Romans 14:19). The book of Proverbs, the great collection of wise sayings found in the Old Testament, also echoes these sentiments: *"A word aptly spoken is like apples of gold in settings of silver"* (Proverbs 25:11 NIV). In other words, kind, uplifting words to people in need are more precious to them than the most costly earthly treasures.

Does speaking such words take much effort? Not at all. But most of us don't think to give them, or, if we do, we don't bother saying them. We need to remember

the "Golden Rule" of Matthew 7:12—*"Therefore, whatever you want men to do to you, do also to them."* Wherever you are in life—whatever you're feeling or whatever you're going through—you can still be someone else's miracle. Focus on the good things of God, and let your heart overflow with His blessings so that you can be a blessing to others!

You may say, "I don't feel as though I have anything to give! I've just been through too much, and I don't feel like blessing anyone right now." We understand

*Focus on the good things of God.*

these feelings, but we also know the incredible power and joy that comes from moving past our own pain and doing all we can to minister and bless others. The apostle Paul understood this, as well. At one point during his life, one of his friends in the ministry—Trophimus—became ill. I'm sure the pain

Trophimus was experiencing caused Paul sorrow. However, Paul knew that, even in his sorrow, he could go on with the work of the Lord and bless others as he ministered to them. (See 2 Timothy 4:20.)

## *Speak It!*

Maybe you wonder who will be the one to bring a miracle to your life in your time of grief and suffering? If no one seems to be stepping up and encouraging you to stand strong in the faith, then I'd like to challenge you to speak it! Speak the miracle yourself. Repeat the Word of God out loud, and meditate on it until it sinks into your innermost being and transforms your life.

This did wonders for Harry and me during our time of mourning. Do you remember how I said we felt plundered, robbed, and destroyed? These feelings are mentioned in Isaiah 42:22, where it speaks of the dire state of God's people—*"But this is a people robbed and plundered; they are all of them snared in holes and hidden in houses of bondage. They have become a prey, with no one to deliver them, a spoil"* (AMP). However, the verse doesn't stop there. It ends by saying that there is *"no one to say, Restore them!"* (AMP). That's the word that Harry and I used to speak a miracle into our own lives. When I would pass Harry in the hallway, I would say, "Restore!" and he would repeat the same thing to me. We continued to do this and noticed that, the more we said it, the more powerful the word became in our mouths. We were prophesying our own futures of restoration. We began to feel our spirits gaining strength, and we became more determined than ever to fight the good fight of faith. We declared that Satan would not defeat us. He was the defeated one; we were the victors in Christ!

So, speak words of healing. Find favorite Scriptures that bolster and expand your faith in God, and say them out loud to yourself and to those who are fighting the good fight of faith along with you. For example, here are some excellent, faith-building verses to keep repeating to yourself:

cs *"Be strong and of good courage; do not be afraid, nor be dismayed, for the* L ORD *your God is with you wherever you go"* (Joshua 1:9).

cs *"You, O* L ORD, *are a shield for me, My glory and the One who lifts up my head"* (Psalm 3:3).

෨ *"I have trusted in Your mercy; my heart shall rejoice in Your salvation. I will sing to the LORD, because He has dealt bountifully with me"* (Psalm 13:5–6).

෨ *"You will show me the path of life; in Your presence is fullness of joy; at Your right hand are pleasures forevermore"* (Psalm 16:11).

෨ *"The LORD is my shepherd; I shall not want. He makes me to lie down in green pastures; He leads me beside the still waters"* (Psalm 23:1–2).

෨ *"O LORD my God, I cried out to You, and You healed me"* (Psalm 30:2).

෨ *"Many are the afflictions of the righteous, but the LORD delivers him out of them all"* (Psalm 34:19).

෨ *"Through God we will do valiantly, for it is He who shall tread down our enemies"* (Psalm 60:12).

෨ *"Trust in the LORD with all your heart, and lean not on your own understanding; in all your ways acknowledge Him, and He shall direct your paths"* (Proverbs 3:5–6).

෨ *"Peace I leave with you, My peace I give to you; not as the world gives do I give to you. Let not your heart be troubled, neither let it be afraid"* (John 14:27).

෨ *"In the world you will have tribulation; but be of good cheer, I have overcome the world"* (John 16:33).

cx "*We are more than conquerors through Him who loved us*" (Romans 8:37).

cx "*I can do all things through Christ who strengthens me*" (Philippians 4:13).

These are just a handful of Scriptures that will help you fill your heart with faith so that you can combat the negative emotions that try to gain a foothold in your mind. Never forget that our feelings have nothing to do with our victory. Whether we feel like standing in faith or not is irrelevant. Whether or not we feel like speaking words of faith does not matter. Our feelings are based on the emotional, but our victory is spiritual. Let your spirit rise up in faith, and stand on the promises of God as you go through the process! *"For I know whom I have believed and am persuaded that He is able to keep what I have committed to Him until that Day"* (2 Timothy 1:12).

# *Points to Ponder*

1. Do you feel as though you are at peace no matter what you are going through? Why, or why not?

2. List three Scriptures from the Appendix that have special meaning to you. Memorize and meditate on these verses so that you can have a greater peace during times of trouble.

   •

   •

   •

3. List people you know who might need some encouragement in their own lives. Pray for these people, and ask God to show you how to minister to them.

## Chapter Three
# A New Battle:

# Knowing Your Limits

### By Cheryl

*T*he summer before Gabrielle went home to be with the Lord, I became ill and started having colon problems. I ignored my own pain because I didn't have time to take care of Gabrielle's medical and emotional needs and also deal with my own symptoms. I reasoned that my body was simply rebelling against the overwhelming pressure I was putting on myself. I was so focused on caring for our daughter that I couldn't bother to think about anything else—even my own health.

On an almost daily basis, I fought intensely painful symptoms. I was often so sick to my stomach that I couldn't eat. Harry became so concerned that he asked a friend who was a doctor about my symptoms. The doctor told Harry that I should be given an exam. Harry

agreed and wanted to schedule an appointment, but I resisted and put it off. I just couldn't leave Gabrielle, even for a couple of hours. I kept thinking how critical it was that her treatment be administered correctly and in a timely fashion, and I felt I needed to be there to do it for her. Every time Harry would bring up my condition and the fact that I needed to see a doctor, I refused. I kept telling myself that it was just the stress I was under and that I would have myself checked out later—that I didn't have time to deal with it now.

Several months went by, and my symptoms grew steadily worse. Harry finally convinced me that a few hours away from my responsibilities to Gabrielle would be good for me. I resisted but finally went. It was so hard to leave my little girl, but I did. After an initial exam, the doctor said that he felt further tests were needed. He suggested that I have an endoscopy and a colonoscopy performed soon. However, the doctor was not overly pressing in his recommendation, so, when I left his office, I told Harry that we didn't need to have the tests done immediately. All I thought about was the amount of time I would have to be away from Gabrielle. The tests would take more time than I could afford to be absent from my daughter's bedside. I truly believed that my symptoms were completely related to stress and my constant lack of sleep. I figured that, as Gabrielle got better, I would get better, too.

## The Battle Continues

Months went by, and, as my symptoms continued, Gabrielle's life on earth was slowly slipping away. When she finally left to be in the arms of the Lord, I felt terribly

sick—in my body and in my heart, as well. The day after her departure, we had her home-going celebration. I felt so broken that I didn't know if I would be able to make it through the services. By God's grace, I made it through. But I was hardly out of the woods yet.

The day after Gabrielle's home-going was Thanksgiving. What was usually a beautiful time with family and friends turned out to be a day of heartache, shock, and confusion. For me, it was also a day of incredible physical pain. My illness hit me with a vengeance, but I assumed that it was simply because of the emotional upheaval I was experiencing.

The next day is when we received our invitations to go to the West Coast to appear on television with friends of ours. My mind and body were screaming at me not to do it. Harry was also feeling intense emotional pain, but we both knew we had to go. We wanted to push ourselves into a better place—a place where we could share our lives, our victories, and our pain with the world around us.

A few days later, on the morning we were to fly to Los Angeles, I was putting makeup on in the bathroom when the most violent wave of nausea hit me. I fell to my knees, feeling as if I had just been hit in the stomach with a battering ram. For a moment, I thought, "I'm going to die right here on the bathroom floor!"

I crawled to the toilet and began throwing up. I didn't care. I just wanted to get rid of all my miserable heartache. I wanted to throw up everything that was plaguing me—the pain, the brokenness, the unbearable and raw wounds of my heart. After all, I felt like God had broken His covenant with me. I felt He had promised

me great things and that He hadn't come through on them. I was brokenhearted over being separated from Gabrielle, and I was also brokenhearted about the seemingly shattered covenant with the precious Lover of my soul, Jesus. Nothing made sense in my life, and I wanted it all to be gone once and for all.

I pulled myself up to my knees, and I declared to Satan, "Devil, you have no control over my life! You cannot kill me! You've had many chances already, and you haven't done it yet. But if you think you can do it, go ahead! Do it right now! Give me all you got because it will never be enough!"

I was having a hard time keeping my mind on what was going on. I just couldn't focus because of the weakened state of my body. Finally, I found enough strength to call out for Harry. "Honey, please come pray for me!" It was all I could say. I felt like I had screamed, but Harry, the lightest sleeper I have ever known, didn't move. I almost hoped that the devil would kill me just to get me out of the horrible pit I was in. I allowed my selfish thoughts to rise up—thoughts of escape from the pain and anguish, from the broken pieces of my shattered life, and from the illness that tortured my body. But I had been walking with the Lord too long to give in. I knew that Satan is a defeated foe. I knew in my spirit that God was not going to let me leave this earth yet. The warrior in me began to rise up.

I remembered that Satan had continually tried to stop me but God made sure that His plan for my life kept moving forward. This knowledge was both a comfort and a torment. I was comforted because I knew that I would never be out of God's will for my life and that

God was in control. But I was tormented because God's sovereignty meant that He had allowed our daughter to be stricken with a brain tumor and that He had allowed her precious little body to go through eleven terrible months before He took her home to heaven.

Finally, Harry heard my whispered screams for help and leapt out of bed. He came running into the bathroom and found me sprawled facedown on the carpet. Obviously confused as to what was happening, he kept asking me what was wrong. All I could say to him was, "Agree with me that this sickness must leave." He immediately began to war for me in the spirit. He rebuked the devil, the sickness, and the symptoms. He came against everything that he could think of and called down the powers of heaven to help us.

My nausea began to lift, and I began to feel stronger. I confessed that Satan would not stop me from getting on that plane. I vowed then and there that I would get on the plane even if I had to crawl. I simply would not let myself be held captive in our home. I knew that was what Satan wanted. He wanted us to stay home and never again go out and minister as a family. He wanted us to remain trapped in the house where our daughter had departed from us. He wanted us to be defeated by giving in to our flesh and our feelings. He didn't stop us, though. We got on the plane that day!

## Facing the Facts

For the next few weeks, I continued to have days when I woke up violently nauseated and threw up. It seemed to happen every five days and finally became a predictable pattern. Our West Coast trip came and

went, and still I suffered from this mysterious illness. Harry again insisted that I see a doctor. But whenever any of our friends who were doctors would call or drop by, they all seemed to agree that my problem was most likely due to physical exhaustion or stress. All of them agreed that it would eventually pass, and I thought so, as well. But it didn't get better; it only got worse. It got so bad that I stopped eating almost completely because I couldn't keep anything in my stomach. Day by day, I got weaker and thinner.

Finally, God intervened by way of a loved one. My sister-in-law and I were taping television shows one afternoon, and I was fighting to keep my composure because of how sick I felt. She knew of my sickness, and she also knew how much I had resisted Harry's pleas to go see a doctor. As soon as we were finished taping, we got into her car and headed for my home so she could drop me off—or so I thought. Instead, she drove to the nearby Cancer Treatment Center of America. She got on her cell phone and phoned a friend there who was a doctor. Then, she called Harry and told him to meet us there.

So, there I was in the doctor's office—finally. The doctor examined me and then ordered a colonoscopy and endoscopy for the following Monday morning. During the intervening time, we ministered in Texas, and I began to talk myself out of undergoing the tests. I once more rationalized that there wasn't anything seriously wrong with me and that I just needed time to heal and some rest from our busy schedule.

There were times that, secretly, I just wanted to get off this planet. I wanted to go to sleep and wake up in

glory. I silently prayed to God to help me do this, but each time, He would draw my thoughts to Harry and the boys and how much they needed me. He would remind me of my calling in life and then gently tell me that I was not finished yet. However, I ignored His whispered words of encouragement and hope, and I continued to give in to my flesh and cry out for escape.

Monday morning came, and Harry took me to the hospital at 7:00 A.M. I tried to resist, but I was so sick and exhausted that I finally just gave in and agreed to have the tests. Being put under for the tests actually sounded good to me, so I quit arguing and went. At the hospital, I drifted in and out of consciousness as I was being prepped for the tests. Each time I came back to reality, I would try to assure Harry that everything was going to be okay. He held my hand as they took me into the test room, where I would soon sleep—a sleep riddled with tormenting thoughts and dreams.

When I awoke in the recovery room, Harry was next to me, holding my hand. Something was wrong, though. He didn't look the same. His face betrayed the fact that he knew something that I didn't. I realized that he looked the same as he did the day he told me that Gabrielle's tumor was in her brain stem. I searched his face for some hint of what could be wrong, but he just sat there silently. When I finally came completely out of the anesthesia, Harry told me the news—the doctors had found a tumor in my colon, and it appeared to be malignant. They had sent off a biopsy of the tumor, and they would know for sure if it was cancerous in twenty-four hours.

In my spirit, I knew this was it. Part of me thought that God had answered my prayers to just take me out

of this world. I told myself that I had run the race, and, now, I had finished the course.

The next day, the report came back. It was confirmed: I had colon cancer. I was to go in for surgery the next morning.

## *"I Am Not Leaving You!"*

The morning of my surgery, I reassured the boys that all was well and that I would see them later. As Harry pulled the car out of the garage, he began to weep. I tried to tell him that it was going to be all right. But they were empty words, and we both knew it. Here I was heading to the hospital for extensive surgery. I honestly didn't care, though. I guess I wasn't even capable of caring. I was emotionally spent and empty.

At the hospital, the nurses gave me a preliminary sedation, and I began drifting in and out as I had during the test procedures. As before, every time I would drift back to consciousness, I would see my precious Harry hovering over me, looking at me for some reassuring word that I was coming back.

As the nurses were wheeling me into the operating room, I was completely out, resting peacefully. Harry later told me that, at that moment, he was getting ready to lean down and whisper in my ear that everything was all right—that if I saw Gabrielle and I wanted to go on to heaven that he and the boys would be okay. He said that, just as he opened his mouth to tell me this, I awoke and spoke to him. What Harry didn't know was that, while I was sleeping peacefully under the anesthesia, the Lord was speaking to my heart. Jesus said to me

then, "I know that you want to come home and be with Me. I know that you miss Gabrielle and that you want to be reunited with her."

The Lord went on, "You have always wanted to stand before Me and hear Me say two words."

I knew in my heart what those words were as the Lord continued to speak to me. "Yes, that's right. You want to hear 'Well done.' But if you come to Me now and stand before Me, you won't hear 'Well done.' You will only hear, 'Well?'"

My mind was foggy, so I asked, "What, Father?"

The Lord spoke to me again and told me that He was not finished with me yet and that, if I chose to come to Him now, I would hear "Well?" instead of "Well done."

I knew that I had to stay. There was no other choice. God knew me well enough to know that I would never willingly disobey Him, no matter how badly I was hurting in my flesh. At that moment, I submitted to His will and made my decision to stay on the earth. With my decision to stay also came a request of the Lord. I told Him I wanted to stay, and I asked for three things. I cried out to Him, "I need my health restored. I need our family restored. And we all need our joy restored."

God heard the cry of my heart, and I felt an assurance that He would grant my requests. It was then that Harry leaned over to tell me it was okay if I wanted to leave for heaven. I opened one eye and looked at him, not knowing what he was about to say (although certainly God did). "I am not leaving you," I said, and then I was out again.

Harry knew that it was settled. I knew it was, too. I would live and not die. There was no longer a choice in the matter. I would be healed. Our family would be restored, and, somehow, our joy would return to us. God would answer my prayer.

I went through surgery and came out with no complications. I began to recover—physically and emotionally. God's answer to my cry while heading for surgery was a start, but it wasn't the end. It did not take away our grief or the brokenness of our hearts. It did not instantly bring closure to the notion that I had thought God was not faithful to us. We would begin again, and we knew that God would restore us eventually.

## Don't Ignore the Warning Signs!

Our bodies are *"fearfully"* and *"wonderfully"* made according to Scripture: *"For you created my inmost being; you knit me together in my mother's womb. I praise you because I am fearfully and wonderfully made; your works are wonderful, I know that full well"* (Psalm 139:13–14 NIV). Even in the New Testament, Paul expressed the value of our physical bodies as dwelling places of the Most High God: *"Do you not know that your body is the temple of the Holy Spirit?"* (1 Corinthians 6:19).

If Scripture puts such a high importance on our physical bodies, then I believe we should, as well. Too often, we are so consumed with helping those we love who are in need that we neglect our own health. Even after a loved one goes to heaven, many people throw themselves back into some activity or work that pushes

their bodies past the limit of wellness. But we need to recognize the warning signs that our bodies give us. We need to know our limits. Our bodies have alarm systems that tell us when something isn't right, just as our houses have alarm systems that tell us when an intruder is present.

We also need to heed the advice of our medical practitioners. They don't suggest tests unless they believe our condition warrants them. We need to learn to trust our doctors, and that in itself is a process. We don't trust doctors just because they are doctors. Trust must be earned. Even after we establish a level of trust with our doctors, we need to take what they tell us and pray about it. The Holy Spirit will guide us into all truth if we will just ask Him.

*The Holy Spirit will guide us into all truth.*

In addition to relying on the medical sciences, we also must recognize the value of time in regard to the healing process. For those of you who feel there is no one to take care of your ailing loved one but you, may I tell you that God can send helpers to aid you? Pray to Him for the help you need. He will answer your prayer. Sometimes, He may send friends or family members to share the burden. Other times, He may prompt you to call on a church, crisis center, or medical center for the help you need. You may hit some red tape and some brick walls along the way, but keep at it until you break through. There is always someone out there who wants to reach out to us in love, whether it is to help with a sick loved one or to help you in the mourning process.

Remember that the price for not taking care of ourselves is the lack of care we will be able to offer to our loved ones. If we don't look after our own health, we will be no good to anyone else. I have found that I am a better wife, mother, and minister when I do what I need to do to keep my physical body in good working order. The same will be true for you no matter what you're facing in life.

## Restoration Is a Process

When we face pain and anguish, our flesh wants out. It's only natural. We want pain to leave as quickly as it came. But therein lies the difficulty. More often than not, the pain we go through is not due to something that happened overnight. Just as the problem didn't arise in a heartbeat, so its solution will usually not be over in a flash. It just doesn't work that way. We must endure the process to embrace the promise.

*We must endure the process to embrace the promise.*

Each person heals at a different rate of time. Recovery—emotional or physical—cannot be rushed. As Americans, we want everything instantly. That goes for Christians in this country, as well. We are so used to having everything readily available to us that we forget the value of patience and steadfastness. Some Christians even believe that, if it doesn't happen quickly, it must not be from God. But that is completely contrary to Scripture. In James 1:4, it says, *"Let patience have its perfect work, that you may be perfect and complete,*

*lacking nothing."* God is certainly patient with us, and we must be patient as well—with ourselves and with each other.

The need for patience is especially important in the beginning stages of the healing process, when it seems as though you will never be happy again. As I just alluded to, some people want immediate restoration and healing in their lives without enduring the process that will lead us from grief to the glory of God's promise of a new day. I can't help but be reminded of when I first learned to swim. Before I married Harry, I had never learned to swim. I actually had an incredible fear of the water—a fear that came from the fact that some of my relatives had drowned in isolated accidents while swimming. However, when our first son was born, Harry and I decided to put a pool in the backyard. We both agreed that I needed to learn how to swim so that I could safely monitor and interact with little Harry while he was in the water.

I remember how Harry started my first swimming lesson. The two of us sat on the steps of the pool in the shallow end, and I got used to the feeling of the water. The next time, we took a few steps into the shallow end. Then, we worked our way up to walking to the middle of the pool. Finally, we walked as far as we could into the deep end. Once I had gotten comfortable walking all around the pool, it was time to actually learn how to swim.

At first, Harry had me tread water in the shallow end. I was happy that he held me up as I learned. It gave me a sense of security and comfort knowing that someone was there to keep me safe. Next, I learned basic

swim strokes. Day after day, I practiced putting my face in the water, kicking my legs, and moving my arms. My first big test came when I attempted to swim from one side of the shallow end to the other. Of course, I wasn't very intimidated by this because I knew that, if I got into trouble, I could simply stand up in the shallow end. I swam from side to side in the shallow end, and then I got ready to leap the last hurdle in my lessons: swimming from the shallow end to the deep end.

*Patience is part of the grieving process.*

On the day I attempted to swim the length of our pool, Harry swam in front of me. He was my safety net and also my cheerleader. He would look back to see how I was doing. When I reached the halfway point, I must have looked a bit scared, because I certainly was! But I didn't quit. I kept going, and, soon enough, I had reached my destination.

My adventure in learning to swim is quite similar to enduring the grief process with patience. In the beginning, you've got to take it slowly and learn to rely on God and others who love you and offer you their support. Little by little, you can begin to move back into enjoying life with a happy and healthy outlook on the future. Eventually, the time will come when you reach the day that you know you are restored and healed. However, if you try to get to that point too quickly or all at once, you'll end up drowning in grief, just as I might have drowned in our pool had I leapt into the deep end on my first day of swimming lessons.

Patience is part of the grieving process that God takes all of us through at one time or another. We can

never embrace the promise if we ignore the process. The author of Hebrews said it this way: *"For ye have need of patience, that, after ye have done the will of God, ye might receive the promise"* (Hebrews 10:36 KJV). That verse reveals the necessity of being patient as we walk with the Lord each day through our times of pain and anguish. How long will we need to keep walking in patience? The answer to that is simple, but not necessarily easy to digest: We walk in patience until we see the fulfillment of God's promise to heal and restore us. However, I can guarantee you that God knows what He is doing! As I mentioned earlier in the book, He knows you, and He has your best interest in mind. He will bring you through your grief at precisely the correct rate for you, so that you will emerge whole and healed.

## Our Loving "Refiner"

Have you ever heard or read the verse that says, *"He will sit as a refiner and a purifier of silver"* (Malachi 3:3)? Harry and I have always been curious as to how this verse relates to our relationships with God. After doing some research and talking to both a silversmith and a refiner of silver, we learned some valuable lessons about just how much God cares for and protects us in the midst of our trials.

In modern times, silver is refined by using chemicals that help separate the silver from the impurities within the metal. In olden times, though, silver refiners would put the metal into a crucible and then place the crucible into a furnace, in the midst of which was a fire heated to more than two thousand degrees Fahrenheit. The refiner would allow the silver to melt in the crucible

as he watched, then, at the right time, he would open a door (or doors) on top of the furnace, and the impurities found in the silver would evaporate upward into the air. Finally, the refiner would peer down at the silver to see if it was ready to be taken out of the fire. How did the refiner know when the silver was ready? He could see his reflection in it.

That's a lot like how God handles us when we are going through trials. He holds us in what we think must be the hottest flames possible. But He never takes His eyes off us; He watches and waits as He sees His image formed in us. If we are patient, we will come out as shining examples of God's love and grace!

I remember a day when the Lord spoke to my heart and told me to look for Him in the midst of my trials. At first, I was puzzled. He went on to explain it to me, saying, "You tend to think that I let you go into trials and trouble alone, that I step away and tell you that I'll see you on the other side when the storm is over."

This kind of an attitude forces us to go looking for the Lord somewhere *outside* our trials. But the Lord spoke so gently to me when He said, "You will never find Me outside the fire. You will only find Me *inside* the fire. In fact, if you look for Me inside the fire, you will find the way through the fire. *'I am the way, the truth, and the life'* (John 14:6). When you find Me, you have found your way through the fire without being consumed."

What a revelation for me to see that God is in the "fires" of our lives and that He is the way through whatever trials we may be facing. The emotional pain we feel from grief can be overcome if we endure the fire. This is a comfort because emotional healing may be the

toughest kind of healing to go through. With physical healing, we can see and chart progress. But emotional healing takes time and is dependent on the individual going through the fires of pain and anguish.

And what fires they are! As we look back, we see things more clearly. We remember the days when the pain finally began to lift. At those times, we could look back and think, "We couldn't have handled the hotter fires three months ago, but now we can see the progress we're making." While we were in the storm, we couldn't see the depth of water that was overwhelming us—until we were on the shore. We couldn't know how close we were to the shore when we were still in the water.

When you are enduring the process, you can't see the depth of what God is doing in your life. But He is doing something—turning what Satan meant for evil into good as He refines you. Look for Him in the midst of your trials, and wait patiently on Him. God has walked with us through every storm we have faced, and He will do the same for you. *"He who has begun a good work in you will complete it until the day of Jesus Christ"* (Philippians 1:6).

# *Points to Ponder*

1.  Have you ever felt as though you were going through something you just couldn't handle? If so, when? If not, what has given you strength to deal with difficult situations in life?

2.  Looking back over your life, think of two times that you endured an intense trial and saw God's mighty hand working in your circumstances. List them here.

    •

    •

3.  Write out a simple prayer that tells God how much you trust Him and lets Him know that you believe He is able to complete the good work He has begun in you. (See Philippians 1:6.)

## Chapter Four
## The Picture:

# Heeding the Voice of the Lord

## By Harry

*A*fter Gabrielle went home to be with the Lord, we made several changes in our house so that we were not constantly reminded of the joy that had been taken from us. We took down all the photographs of her and also all the artwork she had done. It was just too painful for us to look at photos of her or pictures she had drawn. The whole family had believed that God would heal her on this side of heaven, and, now, we were left to ask and answer many incomprehensible questions. The time just after Gabrielle went to heaven was hard enough for us; we didn't want constant reminders of the joy that had been taken from us.

We completely redecorated Gabrielle's room so it did not become some sort of shrine to our daughter's

memory. We replaced the furniture and put in new carpeting. We let Roman decorate it, and it soon became his room. Our bedroom also underwent a makeover, as it was the room where Gabrielle went home to heaven. The visual reminders were just too many, and we wanted a new beginning. Yes, we had fond memories of her, but we did not want to build a shrine.

Gabrielle loved drawing pictures, and her artwork hung on walls throughout the house. Everyone who visited our house became well acquainted with Gabrielle's artistry. Because of that, we decided to send her artwork to all of the people who had participated in her home-going. We wanted these people to know how much we appreciated them, so we sent them artwork that we considered to be of more value than any Rembrandt.

## My "Incomplete" Family

As Cheryl mentioned in the last chapter, we took a trip to the West Coast shortly after Gabrielle went to heaven. In addition to the times of ministry we were able to enjoy, we also took some time out for ourselves so that we could rest a bit and renew our strength. After arriving, we decided to spend a day at Universal Studios Hollywood. In times past, we had all loved going to the theme park, and we looked forward to going back again on this occasion.

It was such a breath of fresh air to see the familiar entrance to the park and get a glimpse of the park's main street just beyond the gate. As soon as we stepped inside the park, a photographer approached us and asked us if she could take our picture so that we could have a memento of our visit. We agreed and lined up

for the photographer, and she snapped our picture. She then handed us a number and told us we could pick up our picture when we were exiting the park later that day.

Soon enough, we were on our way through the park. We had a wonderful time just being together and having some fun as a family. As we headed toward the exit of the park, Roman remarked that we had forgotten to pick up our family photo. We decided that we should at least take a look at the picture, so we headed to the booth where the pictures were displayed. We quickly found our photo, and the boys were excited to see that cartoon characters had been superimposed in the picture alongside us. They were looking at who had been added to the photo, but all I could see was who was missing from the photo: Gabrielle. I wanted to purchase the photo for the boys' sake, but I just couldn't bring myself to do it. I made up an excuse as to why we couldn't buy the picture, and we headed once more for the exit. I left the park that day feeling as if something was missing.

The rest of that night I couldn't get the picture off my mind. It really hit me that day that our family wasn't the same anymore. We had changed, and we would never be the same again. We would never appear complete because our daughter would never again be in a family photo. I vowed right then that I would never again take a family photo. I could not stand the thought of looking at another photograph that didn't have our little girl in it. If our family couldn't be a complete family, I figured, then I didn't want any pictures reminding me of who was missing. For the next year, I refused to have a family picture taken.

## Always in the Family Picture

Normally, we took a family photo at Christmas every year to include in our Christmas cards. The last formal family photo we had taken was with Gabrielle for the Christmas of 1998. Now, two years later, we knew we needed to have another family photo taken. After all, our boys were growing and changing drastically. Young Harry had shot up to six-foot-one, eight inches taller than when we had the 1998 Christmas photo taken. But I resisted getting a new picture taken. I made up every excuse I could think of—the boys needed haircuts, or I needed a haircut. I'd say anything to avoid getting our family photo taken.

One night, Cheryl persisted until we finally did get our photos taken. Most of them were shots of each individual family member; a few of them were of the two boys. When the photographer wanted to gather us together for a family photo, I resisted and won out again. Once more, I succeeded in dodging the memory of our daughter.

Finally, Cheryl went out of her way to plan a family photo session at our house without me knowing it. She set it all up, and, eventually, I found out about the scheduled photo shoot. As the night approached, I knew I had no way out. I began to sulk and get depressed about the whole situation. I had made a vow to never again take another family photo that Gabrielle wasn't in, but I was stuck. I began to ask God to give me a way out of this. The night before we were to have our photos taken, I told God, "I can't do this! It will just bring too much pain." As I sat there dwelling on this and talking to God in my own way, I received an answer to my prayer.

I felt that God was telling me to find the last portrait taken of Gabrielle before her illness and hang it above the mantel over the fireplace in the living room. So, I got up, found the picture, and hung it where God said to.

When the photographer arrived the next evening, he looked over our house from the outside and then came inside, looking for the best place to take the photo. After going through each room of the house, he decided on the living room. When I came downstairs, the photographer had all of his lights set up and had rearranged the furniture for the picture. He gathered us together and positioned us for the photo—right in front of the fireplace.

After I had hung Gabrielle's portrait over the fireplace, Cheryl and the boys had a strong feeling that it was indeed the right time to put her photo back up—that it was the right thing to do for the family. Of course, the boys were already ahead of us in this area. They both had hung their favorite pictures of their sister in their rooms. Harry even had a photo of her hanging above his bed. Now, after hanging the photo in the living room, Cheryl and I knew the time was right for us, as well. The proofs of the photos that arrived a few weeks later proved that the time had indeed been right.

We looked through the photos and began picking out individual shots for our ministry press kits. Then, we came to the hard part—choosing the family photo. As I sat looking at proofs of the family shots, I began to remember what I'd felt in my spirit the night before the photos were taken. When I first heard God tell me to get Gabrielle's photo and hang it above the fireplace, it

wasn't clear to me what God was doing. But as I looked at the photos, I knew. In the family shots, we were all positioned in front of the fireplace. Roman stood next to Harry. Cheryl was seated, and I was standing next to her. Over my shoulder, in clear view, was the glowing portrait of our Gabrielle.

It amazed me how God had orchestrated the whole thing. It was a culmination of many events: Cheryl setting up the photo shoot, my willingness to hang Gabrielle's picture, and the photographer's selection of the fireplace as the background for our photo.

As I sat there gazing at the family photo, the Lord spoke gently to me, "Gabrielle will always be in the family picture—not in the flesh, but in the spirit. She is not dead, but alive!"

For me, it was yet another new day, a new beginning in the midst of the grief and mourning we were enduring, and it all started with a simple act of obedience on my part to listen to what God had planned instead of what I had planned.

## Seek the Lord

When you get to a point where it seems like you can't handle a certain situation, you need to ask the Lord for His help and guidance. Remember that He is the God who will *"instruct you and teach you in the way you should go"* (Psalm 32:8). God is always there for us; we must only ask Him for His help. If I would have gone to God earlier about Gabrielle's photo, He may have guided me then in a way that would have given me peace despite my pain.

This reminds me of a time in the life of David, who became the king of Israel. At one point in his life before he became king, he was on the run, attempting to escape from King Saul, who was intent on killing him. Because Saul was constantly pursuing him, David decided to flee to the land of the Philistines—Israel's hated enemies—and take refuge. While there, David established himself as a warrior of valor and character. One day, he and his men returned to the city of Ziklag, where they had settled among the Philistines. David and his warriors were astonished to find Ziklag in complete ruin. The entire city had been burned by the Amalekites while David and his men were away, and the Amalekite raiders had taken captive all the women and children of the city—including the wives, sons, and daughters of David and his soldiers.

*God is always there for us.*

When David and his men saw what had happened, they *"lifted up their voices and wept, until they had no more power to weep"* (1 Samuel 30:4). Can you imagine how each of them must have felt? The people that had been closest to them had been taken, and David and his men didn't know if their loved ones were even alive. Of course, being the leader, David was an obvious target for blame and soon found himself under attack from his very own warriors. *"Now David was greatly distressed, for the people spoke of stoning him, because the soul of all the people was grieved, every man for his sons and his daughters"* (v. 6). If David didn't already have enough to deal with, now his own "loyal" warriors were ready to shed his blood as payback for what had happened to their families. However, David knew what to do in

moments such as these. He didn't draw his sword and say, "Fine! Whoever wants a piece of me, here I am!" He didn't yell, "You're right! I deserve it!" He didn't fall to the ground, bury his face in his hands, and cry, "O God! How could you let this happen to me? Oh, woe is me!" No! David didn't do any of those things. The Bible says *"David strengthened himself in the LORD his God"* (v. 6).

*Trust in the Lord with all your heart.*

Furthermore, David not only knew where to go for strength but also knew who to turn to for guidance in the midst of his grief and pain—*"David inquired of the LORD"* (v. 8). Because of David's faithfulness, God directed him in what he should do next, and the story ended with David defeating the Amalekite raiders and rescuing everyone and everything that had been taken from him and his men. (See 1 Samuel 30:1–19.)

That is what seeking the Lord can do for someone in the midst of his distress! If you feel as though you are at your wit's end and there is no one who can help you, remember that God is always ready to give you guidance. He won't lead you astray, either. He will lead you down the perfect path of healing and restoration. So, *"trust in the LORD with all your heart, and lean not on your own understanding; in all your ways acknowledge Him, and He shall direct your paths"* (Proverbs 3:5–6).

## Life Awaits You, If...

Maybe you are asking, "What should I do?" Or, maybe you're to the point of asking, "What should I have done?" From my own experience, I can tell you that

there are no exact answers to these questions. We all deal with things differently. We have different response and recovery times. We are not robots, and there is no manual for the process of grief and mourning. Every individual case is different. For you, maybe it would do more harm than good to take down photos of the loved one you no longer have with you. Whatever your particular case may be, God is still there to help you walk through the storm so that, after enduring the process, you can embrace the glory that follows your grief.

Of course, it would be so much easier if we did have some definite rules and prescriptions for the mourning process. But it's just not that easy. We are complex beings, and our reactions to the tragedies of life cannot be measured and timed in some laboratory experiment. Even our flesh is not designed for some rigid time period of recovery. After someone has surgery or begins to heal after an illness, the doctor does not give minute-by-minute instructions for recovery and exact descriptions of how the person should feel and respond. It's more like, "When you feel like you are up to it, you do so-and-so." It's the same way with recovering from grief. We all have to figure out for ourselves what is normal and right for us. How quickly and in what manner we recover will depend on the person, the situation, and the circumstances surrounding the departure of the loved one.

No matter what you're feeling or going through, don't forget that the best any of us can do is to keep going. Now is not the time to give up. Now is not the time to listen to negative feelings that will bring you down if you let them rule your life. Life is just that: life. Even in the midst of our grief, we can be blessed by and even used by God. In fact, after a tragedy, we may be the most

easily used by God because we are broken in our spirits and have come to a place where we are willing to focus our lives on Him and the life that He gives us.

God can use you even in your pain to reach others for His kingdom. But it's up to you. "Life" is spelled with an "if" in the middle. You can have life even in the midst of your grief and pain *if* you choose to live. If you decide to go on, you will go on. If you decide to fall back, you will fall back. If you decide to...you can fill in the rest of this sentence with whatever it is you're struggling with right now. Remember: God has set before us life and death, so *"choose life"* (Deuteronomy 30:19).

*God has set before us life and death.*

## Nowhere to Hide

Have you ever seen a child put his hands over his eyes and declare gleefully, "You can't see me"? Of course, all the while, you can see him perfectly well. That's a lot like when we try to cover up our hurts and pain in the midst of our anguish. God knows how we feel, even if we do try to cover it up and avoid telling Him about what we are thinking or feeling.

The sad thing is that trying to hide our feelings from God hinders our ability to go through the process of grief and mourning. It's so freeing to just get the emotional burdens off our chests by going to God and telling Him how we are feeling. Think about your emotions, and then go to God and give them to Him. Do it before things come to a head, as they did when I refused to have a family photo taken.

Many times, we don't go to the Lord for help because of our stubbornness. We think we can make it through the grief using our own methods. We find it hard to trust that God's plan could be better than ours. But that attitude simply has to go if we are to go on in life. God commanded His children in 1 Peter 5:7 to *"cast all your anxiety on him because he cares for you"* (NIV). In Psalm 55:22, it says, *"Cast your cares on the LORD and he will sustain you"* (NIV).

God has so many resources for us when we are going through pain in our lives, but they will remain unused in heaven if we don't ask Him for help. *"Ask, and it will be given to you"* (Matthew 7:7).

# *Points to Ponder*

1. What are some specific ways that God has directed and guided you in the past?

2. As we saw in this chapter, when David found himself in the midst of a trial, he turned to God. (See 1 Samuel 30:1–6.) Do you usually seek the Lord and His wisdom when you face tough times or tragedies? Why, or why not?

3. List three specific areas of your life in which you desire God's guidance, then pray and ask Him to direct your path. (See Proverbs 3:5–6.)

•

•

•

## Chapter Five

# Through the Sorrow:

# Learning to Embrace the Process of Pain

## By Harry

Everyone who goes through a crisis will eventually come out of it. How they come out of it—broken and defeated, or strong and triumphant—is up to them. Time will tell how we went through the process of pain, either in a healthy, life-building way, or in an unhealthy, destructive way. Think of it this way: When someone breaks a leg, the person can go to a doctor and have the leg set so that it heals properly. The person could also choose not to go to a doctor. The leg would eventually heal on its own, but it wouldn't heal straight.

The tragedies in our lives will pass, but depending on how we deal with the grief and sorrow we feel, we

may end up in an unhealthy emotional state. Cheryl and I both believe that God wants us to approach our sorrow and grief in a healthy way so that, when the time

*God wants us to approach our sorrow and grief in a healthy way.*

of tragedy has passed, we live with healthy emotions. Finding healthy ways to deal with our pain and have our needs met is finding God's best for our lives. While going through the process to embrace the promise, we can always remember that God is with us and is doing a perfect work in us. If we remember this and trust Him through the process, we can emerge from the fires of afflic-

tion without even a trace of "smoke" about us! (See Daniel 3:27.)

## Unnatural Healing

Many times, we fall into the trap of living with and giving into unhealthy emotions during times of grief and sorrow. During these times, those around us may be able to spot the unhealthy ways with which we are dealing with our pain and anguish. While there are many signs that a person is not dealing with sorrow in a healthy way, three main indicators are the most significant and the easiest to recognize.

### Immovable

The first sign that a person is not dealing with sorrow in a healthy way and that proper healing isn't taking place is the person's refusal to leave his home. This is such an easy trap to fall into. It's always easier

to hide at home than face the pain of living life again. We understand this all too well.

After getting out of the house to visit the West Coast, we returned home, and we often felt like we just wanted to stay home. We felt as though we didn't want to deal with anything anymore and we didn't want to have to see anyone again. We simply didn't know how to go on with life at times. Thankfully, two of our friends recognized that we were falling into the trap of becoming hermits.

This couple would actually show up at our home and take us out, even when we resisted. We would say that we didn't want to do anything, but they would step inside our front door and tell us to get ready because we were all going out that night. We would ask where they were taking us. It didn't matter, they said. They were taking us out. Period.

Looking back, we can see just how much our friends did for us. They forced us to break out of our captivity. They broke us out of the prison we had made for ourselves in our own home. As questions, confusion, and grief overwhelmed our thoughts, we began to build walls in our minds and didn't want to face reality again. Our friends helped us break down those walls by showing us the love of Christ in a special way when we needed it most.

Were we better immediately? No, of course not. Grief still clutched at our proverbial throats, and it still tried to strangle the life from us. However, our friends' kind intentions helped us tear down walls that would have surely kept us prisoners to the pain and anguish we felt then.

## Inconsolable

Another major sign of unhealthy healing is a person "parking" in his pain and refusing to rebuild a normal life. After Gabrielle went home, we were confused; our fear of the future was almost too much to bear. The pain and sorrow we felt clouded our minds and numbed us to reality. As a father, I was afraid that, if we went on with life, we would forget what made our little girl so special to us. I thought that we might forget the details—the color of her eyes, the way they sparkled when she talked, and the way she squinted and wrinkled her nose when she laughed. I didn't want to forget how she turned her little head when I whispered to her so she could hear me, or how, if she didn't think I was listening, she would grab me by the head and get nose-to-nose with me so she had my undivided attention. There were so many little things that made Gabrielle special, and I didn't want to leave my place of pain because I believed living life again might cause me to forget them.

Cheryl also struggled in this area. She so badly wanted memories to stay with her that she actually drove to the cemetery after someone told her Gabrielle would be there waiting. She knew it was ridiculous to go, but she still went. She knew Gabrielle wouldn't be there, but she couldn't get past the pain of losing Gabrielle to start living her own life again.

## Impervious

The last major indicator that healing is not taking place properly is when a person feels guilty about being happy in life again. In the midst of pain and sorrow, it is

easy to believe that we don't deserve to be happy again—that we should be impervious to the joy and happiness others are feeling. After all, we reason, our loved ones are gone; why should we ever be happy? Sometimes, we even think it is a disservice to the departed loved one if we find joy in life again.

Obviously, this is not a realistic view of life. Too often, people end up hanging on to guilt, and it becomes almost like a badge of honor. When other people see them in grief, they pity them and give them sympathetic attention. However, this kind of attention does not help anyone going through the grieving process; it only leads a person down a path to deeper depression. Jesus looked at those who suffered with eyes of compassion, but He never pitied them or gave them sympathetic attention. To a man who had been crippled for thirty-eight years, Jesus declared, *"Take up your bed and walk"* (John 5:8). Jesus gave the man a choice. He asked him to choose between living a life of wholeness or continuing to wallow in his pain. Those who are in mourning face the same choice. *"I have set before you life and death, blessing and cursing; therefore choose life"* (Deuteronomy 30:19).

## One Step at a Time

One way to avoid unhealthy healing is to understand some of the basic steps of grief that we all go through during times of sorrow. The following steps were part of the path we found ourselves on during our time of grief. Obviously, the steps do not fall into some tidy little time frame. The amount of time spent on each step will vary from person to person, depending on the individual and the circumstance. In addition, the

steps will probably overlap and may even recur for some people. With this in mind, please remember that these steps represent a fluid process in which nothing is ever set in stone. The only thing guaranteed is the restoration that awaits us *if* we are faithful in following God through the fire.

## Shock and Disbelief

When a loved one departs, we are often hit with the thought of "How could this happen?" Intellectually, we know it happened, but, emotionally, we simply can't accept it. We sit in our sorrow and reason that such sadness happens to other people, but it can't possibly be happening in our lives.

*Restoration awaits us if we are faithful in following God.*

The length of time we remain stuck in this stage is entirely up to us. If we refuse to face reality and deal with the pain, this stage can last for an incredibly long time. Even after just a few weeks, remaining in this stage most likely means that a person is not healing properly and is suffering from unhealthy grief.

Shock is a strange, yet powerful tool in our minds. It can actually help us survive when tragedy strikes. I sometimes wonder if most of us would just lose our minds if the shock of a situation didn't force us to retreat mentally and get a grip on the reality of our situations.

When Cheryl was a little girl, she was in a horrible auto accident. Her family had a head-on collision with

one of the families who lived next door. Cheryl came out of the wreck with a battered body. One of her legs was crushed. Her spine was fractured. Her face had gone through a windshield and required more than one hundred stitches. The neighbors involved in the accident didn't avoid injury, either. In fact, the mother was killed.

At some point later on, Cheryl was told that the mother of the family had been killed in the crash. They told her that the woman had gone to heaven. Cheryl said that she cried and cried, and that her heart was broken. She has told me that she will never forget that moment when she found out that the mother had died. The interesting thing is that this wasn't the first time someone had told Cheryl that the mother had been killed. Others had told her on several different occasions, but her mind would not take hold of it. It didn't register in her mind because she was in such a deep state of shock. But it was the shock that allowed Cheryl to come to a place mentally where she could deal with the reality of the situation.

Shock is much like a breaker box found in a house. When we have too many lines plugged in to the same outlet, our electricity goes out. In the same way, when we are overloaded by too much emotional stress, our minds go into a state of shock that allows us to keep going until we reset the "breakers" in our minds—until we are able to slow down and process all of the emotions that we are feeling and deal with them in a healthy way.

Once the shock begins to wear off and we make an effort to get a grip on things, we can start to process

what has happened. Don't be surprised if you forget many of the details surrounding the tragedy once it is over. The memories will come back with time and with the help of the Holy Spirit.

Remember that shock is a good thing—a mental anesthesia that helps us get a grip mentally before facing reality again. However, don't forget that this is not a place where we should linger in the healing process.

## Expressing Emotion

Another common defense mechanism for dealing with grief is putting up a good front for everyone and stuffing our emotions deep within our hearts. Don't do it! It's not healthy in the least. Let the tears come if you have tears to cry. Don't suppress your feelings. Don't let them control you either, but achieve a healthy balance where you can get things off of your chest and avoid dysfunction and depression.

It's so easy to minimize our pain by burying it. We can tell everyone we meet that we're doing fine. We can keep a stiff upper lip and go about our business as if we are back to normal. Inside, though, our emotions are about to burst open like a ruptured dam.

I'm not saying that you can let down your guard and open up with just anyone. Some people will always be ready to sit in the seat of judgment and tell you how you could be doing things differently in life. I learned this firsthand.

As we were leaving the church to take Gabrielle's body to her final earthly resting place, a man came up to me and offered me a piece of what he must have

thought was great insight. "Well," the man said, "I guess you didn't have enough faith for your daughter's healing."

Remember: We were leaving the church to go the cemetery. We were already in shock. We were already feeling the agony of our daughter's departure. Then, this man decides to judge our faith. It just about knocked the wind right out of me. Honestly, I wanted to lay him out right then and there. Thankfully, I let the Lord lead me instead of my flesh. I pushed aside my rage and asked the man, "Did you pray for my daughter?"

He said, with obvious pride, that he had indeed prayed for Gabrielle.

I asked him, "Then, what does that say about your faith?"

Be careful with whom you share your feelings. Sometimes, people will offer their unsolicited and critical advice whether you open up to them or not. But, if you let the Holy Spirit lead you, He will help you avoid opening up to those people who will do you more harm than good. He will also help you move past the painful comments that others insist on giving to you. If you let these comments get to you, you can be certain that Satan will keep sending critical people across your path to keep you from experiencing healing and recovery.

Don't be afraid to share your feelings with those you love and trust. These are the people who know you better than anyone and with whom you can be yourself. You can safely share your heart and bare your soul with the friends and family whom God has placed in your life. It's healthy to detoxify your soul by letting the tears

flow at times. Don't live in fear of what others think. Do what will bring you to a state of healthy healing and recovery.

Another aspect of bottling up our emotions is the fact that it can lead to physical illness in our lives. Many times, we avoid expressing our feelings because we don't want to feel the pain they cause. But pain is going to come whether you share your feelings or not. If you stuff them down deep in your soul, you will create an incredible strain on your body, and you will eventually suffer for it.

One healthy way Cheryl expressed her emotions was to go into the bathroom alone and talk to the mirror. I'll let her relate what she said in her own words:

> I would go into the bathroom, close the door, and then give the mirror a good piece of my mind. I would express everything that I was feeling. Sometimes, I would lie on the floor and just cry out to God. I would tell Him that I couldn't make it, that I couldn't take it anymore, that I couldn't go on. Then, I would rise from the floor, clean my face, and do exactly what I told the Lord I couldn't do—go on.
>
> I always know that the Savior loves me and that He already knows my innermost thoughts. I know He hears the cry of my heart. I certainly don't make it a habit to cry, whine, or complain because I know these things can be a source of spiritual rebellion in my life. I don't need that. But I also know that my Father God can take it when I need to get something off my chest. He knows me. He made me. He knows when my

emotions are overflowing and about to spill out on the people I love.

## Depression and Loneliness

When we are grieving, we can see the sun, but something keeps us from feeling its warmth. We are surrounded by people, but we often feel isolated and alone. It's as if we are sinking in deep water with the surface in view above us. We see the sky above the water and know that fresh air awaits us there, but we can't push ourselves to do what it takes to get there. Even our friends and family are unable to punch through the depression and loneliness we are feeling in order to help us.

Our family has walked through depression more than once. In the early 1990s, Cheryl went through a fight against depression for nearly two years. When Gabrielle went to heaven, Cheryl felt the same feelings welling up inside her. She was tired. She felt isolated and alone. She was ready to give up. However, she recognized what was happening to her, and she saw a doctor. He was able to prescribe something that helped keep her head above water and deal with the depression and loneliness she was feeling. It wasn't an instant fix, and she never let it become a crutch, but it helped her when she was ready to slip into depression. It was almost like a life preserver that kept her from drowning in her sorrow until she was able to come to grips with her emotions and deal with them in a healthy way.

If you are feeling lonely or depressed, don't worry. It's a natural part of the grieving process. But recognize when your loneliness and depression begins to dominate your life. Seek out help—from family, friends, or

even medical professionals. Life is too good to get stuck wallowing in depression and loneliness. Focus on the future, and move beyond the past.

## Guilt

Often in our grief, we slip into thinking that it was something we did or didn't do that was responsible for the loss of our loved ones. Rarely is this ever the case. Even if we may have been at fault in some way, we can ask God for forgiveness and move forward, keeping in mind that no one can go back and change the past.

Unjustified guilt—guilt that has no basis in reality—is not from God. It is a tool of the devil. It is a state of mind that leaves us hopeless, empty, and confused. Guilt is a prison we build in our minds because of self-condemnation. Satan would love to trap us in this prison and make us think that there is no way out.

*Unjustified guilt is not from God.*

Guilt inevitably comes with grief, but it is not a healthy emotion. We must stop guilt in its tracks if we are to go on with God. Otherwise, Satan will keep us bound in the prison of our own minds. This is a subject that I will explore in greater detail in a later chapter.

## Anger and Resentment

Sorrow often brings with it a very critical spirit. After a loved one departs from this world, we may begin to criticize everyone and everything that had any connection to our loss. We systematically scrutinize the

event and how it unfolded. We want to know why this happened and who is to blame. Blame is a major warning sign that we have stopped in our tracks on the road to healthy healing.

You absolutely must resist the urge to find fault with someone for your loss. You need to watch what you say and how you say it. You need to ask yourself, "Am I focusing on the future or the past?" Resentment grows quickly in our hearts if we do not monitor our motivations and moods.

Don't get me wrong: We may very well feel angry. There's nothing wrong with that, either. Anger is an honest emotion. However, just because we feel a certain way today doesn't mean we should allow ourselves to feel like that forever. We may feel angry for a few days, weeks, or even months, but, eventually, those feelings must be dealt with. Unchecked anger doesn't fix anything. It doesn't do anyone any good, and it only brings harm to the person who is angry. It's like drinking poison in the hope that someone else will die from its effects. What happens? The poison sucks the life out of the one who drank it while the targeted person goes on with life. So, don't let anger control your life. Give it to God. He can take it, as Cheryl pointed out earlier. He's your Father no matter what you say to Him. Let Him know how you feel, even if you are angry with Him, but don't stay angry.

## Resistance to Return to Life

After tragedy has struck in our lives, we like to think that no one else can understand the extent of the loss we've just suffered. We believe that no one can

relate to the pain we are feeling. Everyone around us moves on with their lives, but we sit in our sorrow, alone and determined to make sure everyone remembers us and our loss.

Think about how off-the-wall such emotions are. Everyone has experienced loss. Everyone has gone through painful tragedies. Do we really think we have it worse than anyone ever has? There's always someone who has it worse than we do. If we will break out of the doom and gloom that shackles us, we can reach out to others. Not only will we be a blessing to them, but they will also bless us, especially those who have been down the road of sorrow before.

In Philippians 4:8, the apostle Paul said, *"Whatever things are true, whatever things are noble, whatever things are just, whatever things are pure, whatever things are lovely, whatever things are of good report, if there is any virtue and if there is anything praiseworthy; meditate on these things."* Is this easy to do in the midst of grief and sorrow? Of course not. It may take a lot of effort to fix our minds on something good and positive when all we feel is pain, anguish, and loss. But God is faithful. The Holy Spirit can come to our aid and direct our thoughts to good things; we must only ask Him to. People around us need to see us move on from our pain just as much as we ourselves need to move on from it. Be someone who puts one foot in front of the other and thinks on good things during the journey back into life.

## Hope Returns

Little by little, as we make our way through the initial steps of grief, we begin to see the sun shine

again in our lives. However, even when hope returns, we must keep our faith in God strong. Thoughts of sorrow and grief will linger, and, if they do, it's not something to worry about. But remain hopeful about the future. Focus on moving from grief to glory, and push through the last leg of the process.

Eventually, you will be in a place where you can reach back to those who are suffering loss in their own lives. It's not always easy to share your heart and encourage these people, even long after you've gone through the process yourself. But people will be looking for answers just as you once searched for answers to the tough questions that come after a tragic loss. Your road will become someone else's road, and we must continue to move forward as we move from the process to the promise.

After we had walked down the road of restoration in our own lives, a pastor once remarked to us, "You are comfortable now." We almost shouted at him in disbelief. Comfortable? We felt anything but comfortable—miserable, maybe, but certainly not comfortable. The pastor went on with what he was saying and explained that if you break the word "comfortable" into two parts, you have "comfort" and "able." He said that God had brought us to a point where we were *able* to bring *comfort* to those who were mourning and had no hope or vision for the future.

Looking back, the pastor was right. We are in a position of being "comfort able." We are able to bring comfort to people who are stuck in the miry pit of despair and death. You, too, can come to this place—if you keep your hope for the future and move forward through the grief process.

## *Affirming Reality*

Finally, we come to a place where we can live again and be happy about our lives. The process is over, and we embrace the glory that comes after the grief. To be sure, pain may sometimes singe our hearts like embers of a dying fire. But we are properly healed, and sorrow doesn't control our lives. We are in a place of restoration and recovery. We are able to give comfort to those who are suffering as we once suffered.

This doesn't come easily, nor does it happen overnight. We can very easily get stuck at any stage of grief and wallow in our sorrow. Don't allow yourself to get stuck on the road to recovery and restoration, and don't ever compare yourself to someone else who has gone through the process. Every person heals differently at different rates. There is no right or wrong amount of time for healing. However, it is never right to allow yourself to stop in the healing process.

Victory is never about what we can see or what we are feeling. Victory is always about the faith in our spirits that believes in the promises of God no matter what we see or feel. Cheryl has said many times when preaching that it doesn't matter how we cross the finish line of the grieving process. We may run and leap like a gazelle. We may tiptoe through the tulips or feel as if we're walking on eggshells on the way to the finish line. We may crawl on all fours or even creep on our bellies. How we get there is not important. Getting there is all that matters. When we endure the process, the glory that follows our grief becomes a reality, and we become a tried and true servant of the Most High God. *"When He has tested me, I shall come forth as gold"* (Job 23:10).

## *Points to Ponder*

1. Write down your thoughts on how you are doing in dealing with tragedy or a tough time in each of these areas:

* Getting out of the house and doing things with others:


* Looking to the future and not dwelling on the past:


* Refusing to feel guilty about living a happy life:



2. Nearly all of us have felt, at one time or another, the urge to give in to our loneliness and depression by living in self-pity and believing the notion that no one understands what we are going through. Find three Scriptures in the Appendix that you can memorize to help encourage you in such times, and write them here.

   •


   •


   •

# "Blessed Are Those Who Mourn":

# Finding Comfort through Emotional Release

*By Harry*

God created all of us with the ability to experience emotions. Even Jesus showed His humanity through His emotions. He wept, He rejoiced, and He even let His anger be known a time or two. We experience these same emotions and many others every day of our lives. Sometimes, in the span of just a few minutes, we can experience a whole range of emotions, going from happiness to shock to sadness to confusion. When feelings such as these come, they have an impact on our lives and on the lives of those around us. However, we need emotions, no matter how much they sometimes seem to hurt us in life.

Think about it: A world without emotions would be a cold, dark place. There would be no appreciation of beautiful sunsets, no sense of wonder when a rainbow appeared, no feelings of exuberance when something great happened. Our lives would resemble something like those of robots—just going through the motions.

God knew what He was doing when He gave us emotions. He gave us the ability to experience the grandest of emotions and the lowest of low feelings. We were not meant to be ruled by our emotions, but they still have a valuable place in our lives. Consider how tears are like safety valves that allow the pain, or even joy, in our hearts to run over. The problem is that, somewhere along the way, our society decided that emotions should be kept to ourselves. Now, many say it's not okay to cry in front of others. It's not "nice" to show anger, even in a controlled manner. Basically, we've become a culture of people that "stuffs" our emotions deep within ourselves. This trend has brought new and deadly diseases to our society—diseases that we have no business experiencing because God created us to express our emotions.

*God created us to express our emotions.*

## It's Okay to Let It All Out

When people experience the loss of a loved one, suddenly or after a long period of sickness, the emotions that follow roll in like a tidal wave. Whether the loved one was an infant, a child, a teenager, or an elderly person, the emotions still rise up in our souls violently.

People begin to live on the emotional edge in life, and there is nothing wrong with this. It's normal to experience intense emotions after tragedy strikes. It's a part of the healing process that will take a grieving person from mourning to restoration.

Cheryl and I like to tell people, "Let the emotions out!" It's healthy to let emotions be expressed. We're not supposed to hold them inside. Holding them inside can, and most likely will, make us sick—either emotionally, physically, or both. So, if you need to get angry, get angry. Many times during our mourning, I would stand in front of a mirror and yell, "Why? Why? Why?" Then, I'd turn around and find something to kick. To be sure, sometimes my foot would then be in pain. However, the release of anger brought me a sense of relief and moved me closer to the promise of healing.

Cheryl tended to allow her emotions to be released by crying. Often, it didn't take much to touch something deep inside of her that immediately welled up and spilled out of her. I remember we were once flying in our airplane to a meeting. Cheryl was sitting next to me eating her breakfast. She had a bagel in her hand, and she began to butter it. Soon, she was crying. I looked at her, curious as to why she was crying over a bagel. Then, it hit me: Cheryl used to butter a bagel for Gabrielle every morning. It was an intense memory that could have brought Cheryl a lot of pain had she chosen to stuff the sadness back down into her soul. Instead, she released the emotion and experienced a sweet sense of relief.

If you have experienced the loss of a loved one and are now in the healing process, you are learning to swim in what I call a storm of tears. After the initial

shock dissipates, the tears may come in like a flood. At times, you may feel as though you are drowning in the sorrowful tears that you cry. You may think to yourself, "This will be the death of me. I just can't stop crying! It's too much to handle. Everything I look at or hear makes me cry. It's just too much!" However, a little bit later, the tears will be fewer, even though you are still in pain. Then, they come more infrequently and, finally, not at all, except for maybe a specific holiday or event that brings back some intense memories.

This is a picture of what it's like to walk through the process of emotional healing. The release of our grief must come in some form. Grief is a powerful and intense emotion that cannot be stuffed down without experiencing the devastating effects of doing so. When we suppress our emotions, we are just delaying the process of healing and, at the same time, making our lives miserable—emotionally and, inevitably, physically. If we suppress our emotions today and then continue to do so, they will resurface again later with more intensity than before. Layer upon layer of emotions will eventually erupt in our lives, and we will be forced to deal with them when we have already deteriorated to emotional and physical wrecks.

Suppressing our emotions is not worth it. The pain it will bring to our lives makes it that much more important to deal with our emotions moment by moment. It's much like cutting our lawns. If we tend to the grass when it needs to be cared for, we will be able to maintain a well-groomed lawn. However, if we let the grass grow higher and higher, we will spend an incredible amount of time and intense effort when we finally have to deal with it. So, don't suppress your emotions. Deal

with them little by little. Day by day, you will feel relief as you progress through the process of healing and on toward the glory of a new day free from pain and sorrow.

## Choose Wisely

When we are in private, no one is able to judge or analyze us for our emotional displays. Many times, people don't even understand the depth of what we're feeling. They stand back and say, "Well, she's crying, so she must not be dealing with this very well at all. She must be in terrible shape emotionally." Or, maybe they say something like: "Look at them! They are so angry and bitter. Their anger must be tying them up in knots on the inside." Then comes the lecture: "Your anger is going to destroy you. You need to get some help because you're not handling this very well." Then, these people will generously spend an hour of their time telling you how they would handle the situation, even if they've never been through anything like what you are experiencing. Don't get me wrong: Many of these people mean well, but they don't know what to say. They just feel as though they should say some-thing, even if it comes out in a manner that ends up causing more pain.

When we come in contact with these kinds of people, we often let it hinder our emotional healing by deciding to suppress our emotions whenever we're around others. We feel as though we have enough pain to deal with, so why would we go looking for another lecture about how we need to do this or that to get better? Why should we cry, get angry, be depressed, or be bitter in front of

others when they are going to stand on their soapboxes and preach to us about our pain? Why? Because we need to let these emotions out, or else they will sit in our souls and fester as an open wound would.

What if you are the sort of person who doesn't really need to show a lot of emotion in life? You don't need to cry or kick anything to feel better. You deal with pain in a way that allows you to feel an emotional release in your mind. Even if you are able to do this, you will still run into others who will tell you you're dealing with your grief incorrectly.

These people will see you and talk to you about the cause of your sorrow. Even though you are doing fine and dealing with it in your own silent way, these people get emotional when they talk about your grief. They may cry or even get angry when discussing the passing of your loved one. However, you don't show any emotion in front of them because you have been processing the grief in a different way that is healthy for you. Guess what? Many times, these people will say that you're dealing with the situation all wrong. They may say that you are in denial because you don't show any emotion. They may even say that you should be angry at God because they certainly would be if they were in your shoes.

So, on the one hand, there are those people who will criticize you for showing emotion. On the other hand, some people will tell you that you are wrong not to show any emotion. If you find yourself going through either of these scenarios, may I suggest something to you? You are spending too much time with the wrong people! My guess is that the people who are responding in

these ways are not those who are intimately acquainted with you and who understand your methods of working through grief. They are not those who have seen you fighting the good fight of faith every day. They are those who simply come in to your life on any given day, observe your actions, draw their own conclusions, and then proceed to give you their opinions—sometimes because they are trying to help, and sometimes because they think they know better than you do.

We must be sensitive about whom we share our feelings with in public. Not everyone is mature enough to handle an emotionally charged encounter. Does that mean we should shy away from sharing our feelings at all? Of course not. We must find a way to release our emotions, and baring our souls to others is an excellent and God-given way to do this. Talking to others will help us process the pain we are feeling. When we

*God is always big enough.*

drive our feelings underground, we put ourselves in a place of impending destruction. So, no matter how you share your feelings, pray that God would lead you to others who will be there when you need a shoulder to lean on or cry on. It may be an individual—a family member, a friend, or maybe a pastor—or it may even be a help group. Some groups specifically deal with getting through grief. These groups can be an excellent way to process your emotional pain because everyone in the group is dealing with the same thing. Amazingly enough, the atmosphere in these groups isn't somber and sad. Instead, it's a place of healing where people are open and honest with each other. It's a place where

people can find a healthy way to deal with the emotions they face.

Of course, the first place we can turn when we need to unload our feelings is God. God is always big enough to handle whatever we take to Him. He'll wait patiently for us to rant and rave or cry and wail, and then He'll whisper His words of sweet peace in our souls. Go to Him in prayer, and seek His face. Ask Him to show you Scriptures that will help you deal with your emotions. Ask Him to minister to your emotional needs through the power of the Holy Spirit. He's a good God. He'll meet you where you are if you will ask Him. *"And you will seek Me and find Me, when you search for Me with all your heart"* (Jeremiah 29:13).

## Patience Is a Virtue

As both Cheryl and I have stated already, everyone heals at a different rate. Some of us are able to deal with and process grief more quickly than others. For those of us who have family members who are also processing grief in their lives, we need to be sensitive to their timetables for healing.

Cheryl and I progressed through the healing process at a similar rate. For you, maybe it will be different. Maybe your spouse, siblings, parents, or children will need more time than you. Give them all the time they need as long as they are experiencing a healthy grieving process. Remember: There is no hurry to get through grief. The key is to get through and come out on the other side a whole and healed person. Therefore, we need to remain patient with those closest to us if they need longer periods of time to process their own grief.

Many family situations are volatile enough that we don't need to add fuel to the fire by speaking rashly in times of grief. Careless words spoken to those who are emotionally tender can carry an incredible weight of guilt or condemnation. Family members may begin to think that we blame them for the loss of the loved one, or that we don't respect or love them as much as we did before the grieving process started. Words spoken to loved ones who are grieving will never fall on deaf ears.

Words that are spoken during times of mourning are apt to stick with a family member for a long time because of the highly emotional state everyone in the family is in. Critical and mean-spirited words can last for a lifetime if care is not taken to what is said. If we speak such words, we will bear the brunt of the hurt person's feelings toward us. We may not have meant the words to sound mean or critical, but they sometimes come across that way nonetheless. Therefore, we must think hard before we speak and consider whether or not what we are saying could hurt the person we're talking to. Don't be afraid to try to motivate and encourage your loved ones in times of grief. However, do it with a gentle spirit and words that are positive, uplifting, and full of faith and mercy.

## Monitor Your Progress

As I've said, we need to release our emotions if we are to experience complete healing from our grief. However, we can let our emotions control our lives if we are not monitoring our progression in the healing process. Take crying, for instance. As I mentioned earlier, tears will often flow like a river after the passing of a loved one. Little by little, the tears should diminish until they

nearly disappear altogether. If you find that you are still crying uncontrollably months after the departure of your loved one, you need to sit down and really think about whether or not you are allowing your emotions to control your life. You need to examine how you have been dealing with your emotional grief.

It is easy enough to generate tears by way of our thoughts. Hollywood has helped us do this for years, prompting us to cry about people we don't even know and situations with which we are not even involved. Therefore, it is critical that we take control of our thoughts. Remember, we are in control of our minds; they are not in control of us. If you are allowing thoughts to rise up and trigger emotional outbursts, then stop and think about what you can do to keep yourself from falling prey to this tendency. In the next chapter, Cheryl will deal specifically with how to fight the battle of the mind.

Remember that healing and restoration is a process. If you monitor your own progress in this process, you can maintain a steady advance toward complete healing. Your journey may and probably will take you through many tears and outbursts of anger and bitterness, including the need to physically release these emotions. Don't worry! Healing is on the way. Emotional release is a good sign that you are dealing with your grief in a healthy and positive way—a way that will bring you the comfort you so dearly need. *"Blessed are those who mourn, for they shall be comforted"* (Matthew 5:4).

## *Points to Ponder*

1.  a. In this chapter, we came to understand the importance of expressing our emotions when we are dealing with tragedy. If you tend to suppress your emotions, why do you feel as though you can't express yourself?

    b. If you usually have a hard time keeping your emotions in check, what are some things you can do to express what you are feeling in a more healthy way?

2.  a. Think about the people with whom you spend most of your time. Are they encouraging you or dragging you down? In what ways?

    b. What are some things you can do to spend more time with people who encourage you and less time with those who drag you down?

# The Mind's Eye:

# Coping with Mental Anguish

## By Cheryl

One of the most difficult and heartbreaking things I had to deal with as Gabrielle's mother after she went to heaven was the constant replaying of images of her in my mind. At first, I was in so much pain that I didn't realize how inaccurate these images were, and I fell prey to Satan's continued efforts to cause me pain.

On a spiritual level, the images that flashed before my mind's eye didn't represent who Gabrielle is. (I say "is" because she's alive and well in heaven!) I initially failed to realize that I needed to separate the eternal, spiritual side of Gabrielle from the physical images of her in my mind. We easily forget that we are spiritual beings, and we think that our physical bodies make

up who we really are. We can't "see" our spirits with our natural eyes when defining who we and others are, so we naturally put more emphasis on the flesh. However, we are who we are for eternity. When our physical bodies pass away, we're still alive—our spirits still exist. We shed our fleshly bodies, and we live on in eternity. We don't become someone else. We are who we were on earth, just without the body. It's a simple fact, but it's a hard one to remember when a loved one passes on.

It gives me comfort to know that God created us to change into a better state of being when we go to be with Him in heaven. We shed our mortal flesh and live on as eternal spirits. It's almost like a caterpillar becoming a butterfly. A caterpillar looks more beautiful and exquisite *after* it becomes a butterfly.

It's hard to look at ourselves and each other from God's perspective. He gave us such a wonderfully complex earthly body that we mistakenly think that our flesh is the true essence of who we are. God did such fine work in creating our earthly bodies that it's hard to imagine that anything better could await us. But God does have something more stunning in store for us, and it surpasses the grandeur of our physical bodies.

This is what we must remember after a loved one passes on. The images we see of them in our minds are pictures of who they were on earth, not who they are right now. Satan wants to keep us focused on the wrong reality. When I remember and focus on who Gabrielle was at the end of her life instead of who she is right now, I am falling into a trap of the devil. Yes, Gabrielle did have a physical body at one time on earth, but that wasn't *who* she was and is. When she went to heaven,

she graduated into a state that is more godlike than ever!

## *Robbed?*

When Gabrielle went home to be with the Lord, I couldn't help but think that she had been robbed of her time on earth. She was robbed of being a child and experiencing all the adventure and fun that comes with it. She was robbed of maturing into a teenager, getting her first car, going on her first date, getting married, and having children of her own.

Then, I began to feel that we were also robbed of all the joy that she, as our little girl, would have given to us. There would be no mother-daughter talks, no special activities like baking together or staying up late watching movies. There would be no special day for Harry when he would walk her down the aisle and give her hand to the man of her dreams.

All of these thoughts, though, were my flesh speaking and my flesh hurting. Gabrielle's flesh wasn't hurting. Our feelings were the ones hurting, not hers. We felt separated from her, but there was no separation for her. She was—and is—in a place free of physical and emotional pain, and any feeling of being separated. *"And God will wipe away every tear from their eyes; there shall be no more death, nor sorrow, nor crying. There shall be no more pain, for the former things have passed away"* (Rev. 21:4).

Harry and I entertained these thoughts of being robbed for several months, and then it finally occurred to us that we had been looking at our loss from a

human standpoint. We hadn't been viewing things as God would. All we could think of was that Gabrielle was gone, but we began to recognize the fact that she is still alive and living in heaven with Jesus. Gabrielle is in the loving arms of our Father. She will never again have to go through the pain, problems, and disappointments that we all face on earth. She wasn't robbed of anything. In heaven, she is happier than she ever was or could have been on earth.

Our outlook changed when we started seeing things from God's perspective—the perspective that takes into account that *"to live is Christ, and to die is gain"* (Philippians 1:21). When we took hold of that revelation, we discerned where the painful images in our minds were coming from—the Prince of Darkness. Satan always shows us mental movies of negative things that bring us despair, but God brings images of love, light, and hope to our minds.

*To live is Christ, and to die is gain.*

The images God gave us of Gabrielle brought us peace and comfort. We remembered in celebration her life of love, service, and giving with the knowledge that her life hasn't ended. We came to a place where we were able to thank God that He "loaned" us the precious gem of a girl for the few years she was here on earth. We thank Him for making such a unique and special individual and for allowing us to share our lives with her.

We may have initially felt robbed, and our flesh cried out in pain. But, once we finally understood that Gabrielle was better than just "all right"—that she was in

heaven—we took comfort in the fact that she was no longer only in our past. She is in our future. Now, we can look back on that November day and remember it as the day that our little girl was walked down the aisle and given over to the only man good enough for her— Jesus Christ, her Savior and Bridegroom.

## That's What Friends Are For

As we mentioned previously, we had friends who were determined to keep us from making our home a prison. It seemed as if they were on our doorstep every day, ready to take us to lunch or dinner or a movie— anywhere but home.

Our friends knew how badly we needed to get out, even if we didn't want to go. Part of the reason for our reluctance to go out was the fact that we knew we would be in a position of emotional vulnerability in front of others. After saying goodbye to a loved one for the last time on earth, everything from that point on seems to remind us of him or her—a song on the radio, a certain fragrance, a smile, even a particular word. It's as though our minds are able to dredge up some memory in reaction to whatever we're seeing, hearing, tasting, smelling, or touching. The memories can be so intense that they overwhelm us. Most of us don't want to be around others when this happens, so isolation seems to be the best answer. However, it is not the answer; it is a death sentence to our futures. It will lead to devastation and destruction in our lives.

When friends and family want to help you through your sorrow by getting you to live life again, do it! Will the memories creep into your mind? Probably so.

But life will go on around you whether you choose to start living it again or not. The memories may be there, and it may be difficult to deal with them, but isolation is simply out of the question if you really want to be restored and find recovery. Find a reason to live again when your friends and family encourage you to get up and get moving!

## The Devil Is Still a Liar

John 8:44 says, *"When* [the devil] *speaks a lie, he speaks from his own resources, for he is a liar and the father of it."* Satan loves to come to us in our grief and tell us that no one has ever had it as bad as we have it. He encourages us to think the worst and to believe that there is no one to help us, that no one loves us.

He's a liar!

He always has been a liar. Do you really think that the children of God are ever without Someone who loves them and wants to provide for them when they're hurting? It's just not true. We always have resources because the Lord is a loving, all-powerful God who wants to bless His children. We can go to God for guidance and let Him speak to us in our sorrow. We can also find out from Him the best ways of dealing with our grief.

Of course, the first place God usually points us to is the Bible. The Bible is full of life-giving words from the very lips of God and His chosen vessels of the past. Immerse yourself in the Bible. Let it sink into your mind and your spirit until there is no room for the lies of the devil.

Don't refuse the guidance of God, and don't try to replace His answer to your grief with something the devil wants to give you. Don't rely on food, alcohol, drugs, television, movies, or anything else as a comforter in your time of sorrow. We have the ultimate Comforter in the person of the Holy Spirit. (See John 14:16.) Don't put anything else ahead of the Holy Spirit, making it a "god" in your life. God must be first in our lives. He is the answer—*"the way, the truth, and the life"* (John 14:6). If we put Him first in our lives, He will guide us and send us wise and godly people who can help us.

Also, don't refuse to seek out help. We're not supposed to be loners in life, and, when tragedy and sorrow strike, we especially need a support network around us. As we just discussed, our family and friends can be of incredible value to us in our grief. There are also many crisis centers that can help us through the painful memories and images that will inevitably come to us; groups that focus on getting past grief; pastors who can minister to us from

*If we put God first in our lives, He will guide us and help us.*

God's Word; and medical professionals, such as Christian psychologists, who can assist us in our recovery. Of course, when seeking any help, be sure you have clear guidance from God so that you can find someone who understands you and your Christian worldview from a spiritual standpoint.

Don't listen to the lie of the devil that no one can help you through your sorrow. You may not be in the mood to search for help, but it's there if you want it.

Remember that *"two are better than one, because they have a good reward for their labor"* (Ecclesiastes 4:9).

# Never Forgotten

One of my prayers after Gabrielle went home was that people would remember her and the life of service and love that she lived. God answered this prayer in a dramatic way when He showed me the legacy our daughter had left behind.

We were ministering in Alabama, and, after one of the services, a little girl approached me.

"I know who you are," she said.

I smiled at her. I had been getting similar comments ever since I won the Miss America pageant. She hesitated for a second, then said quickly, "You are...you are...you are Gabrielle's mama!"

What a surprise! Harry and I had been so concerned that people would forget our vivacious and anointed daughter. We knew that many had been touched and blessed by her ministry, but we were sad that her ministry had been lost to so many others who had never seen or heard her.

When this precious little nine-year-old girl came up to me and said I was Gabrielle's mother, I could hardly believe my ears. She was so excited—not to meet a former Miss America, but to meet the mother of beautiful Gabrielle Christian Salem. Harry and I didn't know that God had already made a name for our daughter throughout the world of the faithful. God helped me understand this by having someone write me a letter that included part of Hebrews 11 in it.

Hebrews 11 is the famous "Faith Hall of Fame" chapter. In it, many of the great men and women of faith are listed to encourage the reader. In Hebrews 11:13, it says, *"These all died in faith, not having received the promises, but having seen them afar off were assured of them, embraced them and confessed that they were strangers and pilgrims on the earth."* Every single one of the great heroes of faith died without having received the promise of the Messiah on this side of heaven. But think of the legacy they have left us! Their lives of faith have impacted God's people for thousands of years.

I had never thought about Hebrews 11 in this light. Instead of feeling guilty and condemned about the loss of Gabrielle and her ministry, I began to understand that God is only interested in each one of us running his or her course in life. Gabrielle had run her race and finished it—much earlier than I would have ever imagined,

*It's all in God's control.*

but that's when her race came to an end here on earth.

We need to recognize that we don't understand everything on this side of heaven. The Bible is clear that *"it is appointed for men to die once"* (Hebrews 9:27). It's not up to us, and it's certainly not up to the devil. God determines the appointed time for our passing from this world. If we are living a life of faith, we don't need to think about when our time will come or why someone else went sooner than we expected. It's all in God's control. I think children have an easier time with this because they have such a simple, trusting faith. Our son Harry kept asking Harry and me why we cried so much after Gabrielle went to heaven. He asked us over

and over, "Don't you believe that she is in heaven?" He had a basic understanding of the situation that we were hindered from seeing because of our "need" to understand why our daughter was no longer with us.

If Harry and I had dwelt on the sorrow that pierced our souls, we would have never "seen" the rest of the picture God was painting for us. We would have missed out on picturing Gabrielle happy and healthy in heaven. Remember that God's perspective is always different than ours. A heavenly view of things is much clearer than any view of things from an earthly standpoint.

One day, as we were getting a glimpse of this revelation in our lives, I heard the Lord say, *"I am the way, the truth, and the life."*

I knew very well that this was found in John 14:6, so I acknowledged this in my mind and said, "I know that, Lord."

The Holy Spirit said, "When you know this, then you will stop looking for Me outside every fire (every trial) in your life."

The light of God's revelation hit me then. It shone so brightly in my spirit that I knew I would never again face another problem without Him and without being able to look at things from His perspective.

## *Work through the Pain*

In our society, nurses will get us up out of bed within a few hours after some types of surgery. They will ask us to walk up and down the hall so we can exercise our bodies—even though it causes us pain.

Medical professionals did not always believe in this sort of treatment, choosing rather to allow patients long periods of bed rest before asking them to move. Today, that thinking has completely changed. It has been discovered through the years that patients recover much faster if they start moving soon after surgery.

In the same way, after Gabrielle's passing, Harry and I knew we needed to get back to our calling in life—ministering—even though it caused us pain, both emotionally and physically. Even the Bible says that we should *"pray for one another, that you may be healed"* (James 5:16). What's interesting is that this verse is talking about praying for others who need healing. However, it's clear that the meaning of this verse is to tell us that, as we pray for and minister to others and they pray for and minister to us, we too will experience healing.

*As you bring healing to others, you will find healing for yourself.*

Do you want to be free from the mental pictures that keep assailing your mind? Then get back to work! Get back to living life and ministering to others in whatever way God has called you to do. As you bring healing and recovery to others, you will also find healing and recovery for yourself.

## *Your Mind Won't Quit Talking?*

There will certainly be times when the images that run through our minds seem like a flood that can't be stopped, especially right after a loved one goes home. At

those times, it seems impossible to heed the words of the apostle Paul in Philippians 4:8:

> *Whatever things are true, whatever things are noble, whatever things are just, whatever things are pure, whatever things are lovely, whatever things are of good report, if there is any virtue and if there is anything praiseworthy; meditate on these things.*

When our minds are running in circles and the images of our loved ones keep overwhelming us, we may wonder how we could ever fix our minds on anything good. In those times when it seems most difficult, there are some steps we can take to stem the tide of our minds.

## Triggers

First, we can think about what triggers these memories. It may be something like shopping in a certain department in a store, driving down a particular stretch of highway, or even the way a specific towel is hung in the bathroom. Eventually, these triggers may be used to bring back wonderful memories—but not when we are fighting to keep the images out of our minds during intense grief. During those times, discover and recognize what triggers the memories so you can figure out ways to stop these images in their tracks.

## Draw the Line

After we have determined what triggers these painful images, we can decide to avoid them by doing whatever it takes to stay away. Remember that we are in control of our minds—not the other way around.

Draw the line before these memories can enter your mind, and avoid the triggers that bring them rushing back to your thoughts.

## Focus on the Good

It may be difficult—actually, it *will* be difficult—but we can consciously make an effort to focus our minds on the good things in our lives, just like the apostle Paul urged us to do in the verse we just looked at.

Don't wait for good things to happen so you can think about them then. Actively recall, or even create, good and pleasing thoughts in your mind, and stop painful images from sneaking back into your thoughts.

## Keep Reframing

People who overcome grief or other trials in life are what I call master "reframers." When we reframe something in our minds, we look at it from a different perspective—we actively look for good despite the bad in our lives. Reframing can bring us peace in the midst of life's storms. Some people call this looking for the silver lining in every cloud. Whatever you like to call it, it is a powerful way to keep our minds from focusing on the pain and anguish we feel. It releases our minds and spirits to look at things afresh from God's point of view.

## Block It

No matter how many precautions we take to avoid facing painful images, every so often they will inevitably slip past the defenses we have created. In those

instances, we need to shut the image down and block it out of our minds by replacing it with something else. If it won't go away, try to put a positive spin on it by reframing it.

Negative and painful thoughts will come from time to time, but you don't have to let the thoughts remain. If such thoughts do come, don't entertain them. Focus on blocking them out and replacing them with positive, godly thoughts.

When the Israelites entered the Promised Land to live there, they first had to defeat the heathen of the land. Only after they dispossessed the inhabitants of the land could they settle down and live in peace. This is how we need to approach dealing with the painful images that come to us. We need to dispossess the "heathen" of our minds—negative and painful thoughts—and then settle our minds with peaceful and good things. It's always up to us.

The choice is yours: You can react to the pain that comes your way, or you can proactively fight the good fight of faith and watch the Lord work in your life. *"The righteous will live by his faith"* (Habakkuk 2:4 NIV).

## *Points to Ponder*

1.  What are some recurring thoughts that keep your mind focused on the tragedy or trial you are going through?

2.  List three thoughts, memories, and/or Scriptures that you could use to replace negative thoughts when they assail your mind.

    •

    •

    •

3.  Write out a prayer in which you ask God to help you keep your mind on pure and holy things, then thank Him for guiding you in this area.

# Good-Bye, Guilt:

# Quieting the Voice of the Flesh

## *By Harry*

God has been a vital part of our lives for many years. Cheryl and I have loved and trusted Him in everything we've done. Yet, when Gabrielle went to be with Him, we found ourselves crushed by an overwhelming weight of guilt on a daily basis, and we felt like there was no way out. It seemed as if there was something more we could have—or should have—done for our daughter. Did we not have great enough faith? Should we have tried another form of treatment when her condition began to deteriorate more rapidly?

We knew that God was not responsible for this unjustified guilt we felt. It had nothing at all to do with Him. Guilt and the hopelessness that comes with it are from Satan. If we allow guilt to sit in our minds and

continue to foster an attitude of self-condemnation, guilt will become a prison. It will dominate our minds to the point where we can't even begin to comprehend a way out of the pain we're in.

We knew very well that guilt's effects could lead to self-destruction and that we shouldn't feel guilty. But we still did. The same guilty feelings common to everyone after the loss of a loved one crept into our minds. At times, we felt as though we would never be able to get out from under the guilty feelings. We also knew, though, that feelings couldn't control our lives—unless we allowed them to do so.

Day by day, Cheryl and I battled the guilt that welled up in our minds and spirits. If that wasn't enough, we faced harsh and critical words from people who seemed intent on making sure we felt guilty. Anonymous e-mails and letters mercilessly accused us of many things. Some people let us know that if we hadn't put Gabrielle on medication, she would still be alive. Others accused us of not having enough faith for our daughter's healing. We didn't receive a lot of these mean-spirited messages, but it only took a few to cause our already guilty minds to spin out of control in a state of self-condemnation.

A handful of our ministry services were also cancelled with no explanation given. These few places that took us off their schedules refused to talk to us or even give us a reason. It was so easy to feel like they were judging and blaming us, and it was like adding fuel to the fire of guilt in our minds. Our minds kept rehearsing all the "What ifs"—what if we would have tried another treatment, what if we hadn't given her this drug, what if we had tried that drug? It was a

never-ending cycle of questions that we couldn't possibly answer.

Every day, we dealt with the guilt that came from trying to answer such questions. We knew the key was to bring it down in our minds and not let it grow worse. We understood that we had to bring *"every thought into captivity to the obedience of Christ"* (2 Corinthians 10:5) and renew our minds in Christ (Romans 12:2). Was it easy? No, but it was certainly achievable through the power of the Holy Spirit working in us.

## Guilt from Another Perspective

One of the strange things about guilt is that each person looks at it differently. Guilt is guilt, to be sure, but I found it interesting that someone looking at our situation could have such a different view of everything than us.

A little while after Gabrielle had gone home, I was talking with a man about the tragedy we had just gone through. He commented that we had eleven months to spend with her before she left and that we had even had a chance to say our earthly good-byes. He went on to mention some of the other tragedies that had recently occurred in our town. One family had lost a child in an auto accident. Another child had killed himself with a single gunshot. He then reflectively asked which of all these tragedies was the worst? Could any be worse than one of the others? The man I was talking with thought so. He said he based this belief on one thing—the guilt that came after the tragedy had occurred. Parents may feel guilty about a child who dies in an auto accident because they may have been driving, or the child might have been

driving a car that they had bought for him. Suicides are particularly hard to deal with because parents automatically take responsibility for the quality of life, or lack thereof, that their child had before ending his life.

But, I said, what about Gabrielle? It wasn't like these other people had more right to feel guilty than Cheryl and I did. She was our flesh and blood. The cancer that finally sent her to heaven could have come from *our* bodies. It was enough to make me feel as guilty as any other parent who lost a child in a radically different situation. After all, they lost their children in the blink of an eye. Cheryl and I had to watch our daughter suffer for eleven months, her body deteriorating little by little until the painful end. However, even that kind of thinking is dangerous because it judges one person's tragedy against another's. The bottom line is that tragic loss forces those involved to face the guilt that inevitably comes.

## What to Do with Guilt

Our greatest victory in our struggle to overcome guilt was when we acknowledged the fact that God is God and that He has everything under control. In Romans 8:28, it says that *"all things work together for good to those who love God, to those who are the called according to His purpose."* If we really believe the words of that verse—that God is working everything in our lives for good—then there can be no room for unjustified guilt. If God knows best, then things happen for a reason, even if we can't understand them or even if we didn't want them to happen. Simply put, it's out of our hands. Everything surrounding what happened to us was not under our control.

We may believe that God is in control. We may confess it in prayer. We may sing it during praise and worship. We may try to live like it every day as we go about our business. However, as soon as something comes along in life that we don't like, we act like *we* are in control. It's like saying that God is behind the wheel of our lives until tragedy and trial strike, then we take the wheel back from God and try to do things our way.

When guilt and condemnation overwhelmed us and we tried to figure everything out for ourselves, it was as if we took the reins of our lives and pushed God aside in our quest for answers to what had happened. Finally, one day, Cheryl rose above the weight of the guilt and told God, "It is not about us. It is about You, God! We trust You, even when we don't understand. We trust You when we have no answers to the questions screaming through our minds. We trust You for eternity. We don't have to understand 'why' to be able to go into the future without guilt or condemnation!"

This simple prayer of trust and faith was a major breakthrough for us. It was a revelation of God's sovereignty that pulled us up from the guilt we were drowning in. From that point on, we were able to deal with the guilt and condemnation that tried to assail our minds day by day, remembering that *"there is now no condemnation for those who are in Christ Jesus"* (Romans 8:1 NIV).

## Consider the Source

As Christians, we may know and understand that unjustified guilt does not come from God. When we begin to experience feelings of such guilt, we must be sensitive

enough to know where the pain is coming from. Satan is the author of all that is dark, evil, and depressing in life. When we recognize where negative influences come from, we can better fight against them by praying and directing our focus on drawing closer to God.

Many times, we feel guilty simply because we want to blame someone and there is no one else to point the finger at. In our culture, it's almost as if we feel irresponsible if we don't feel guilty about tragedy. It's like feeling guilty is some saintly duty and that, if we don't feel guilty, we're not really good people. That's a lie from the devil! God doesn't want us to feel guilty about something that we had no control over. If there truly was something we did wrong, we can be sensitive to the Holy Spirit's conviction, ask God for forgiveness, and get on with life. No matter what the situation, unjustified guilt is pointless. It does not move us forward into life; it only drags us down into depression.

## What's Done Is Done

Another reason we may feel guilty after a tragedy is that we didn't do enough. Maybe it's because we always want to do our best that we feel this way. In any case, the fact is that it's over. There is nothing more we can do, even if there was something more we could have done. Dwelling on it now only leads to greater and more depressing feelings of guilt and condemnation. People who are the happiest and healthiest in life are those who leave the past behind and do not allow it to bring them down with guilty regrets.

In the movie *Schindler's List,* there is a scene during which those who were saved by Schindler are paraded

past the camera. Instead of looking at all of these people with pride, Schindler took off his wedding ring, looked into the camera, and said, "I could have saved two more people if I had given up my wedding ring!" This man, who had given of himself so unselfishly, still was tortured by the idea that he could have done more. The guilt that Schindler allowed himself to feel was completely unjustified. His example can help us better understand and move past unjustified guilt caused by the thought that we should—or could—have done more.

Instead of focusing on what we did not do, we should think about all we were able to do while our loved ones were still alive. This isn't so we can puff ourselves up in pride. It's simply a way of focusing on the beautiful and unselfish things we were able to do instead of dwelling on what else we could have done. We can fill our cups with these wonderful thoughts and hold them close to our hearts.

## Fight the Flesh

Fighting guilt is just like any other fight of faith—it comes down to warring against the flesh and rising up in the spirit. *"For we do not wrestle against flesh and blood, but against principalities, against powers, against the rulers of the darkness of this age, against spiritual hosts of wickedness in the heavenly places"* (Ephesians 6:12). God will aid us in this process, but it's ultimately up to us whether we will believe the lie of the enemy or trust in God and His plan for the future.

There is a story of a farmer who had a beautiful piece of land that was covered with rich crops. One day,

someone remarked to him, "God sure gave you beautiful crops!" The farmer looked reflectively out over his fields and then said, "That's true, but you should have seen it when God had it all by Himself!"

God certainly provided the farmer with the rich soil and the right climate with which to grow his crops, but the farmer had a major role, too. He was the one who had to break the land, plant the seeds, weed the ground, and care for the crops as they grew.

What does this have to do with overcoming guilt?

In 2 Peter 1:3, it says, *"His divine power has given us everything we need for life and godliness"* (NIV). God has given to us all that we need to live a rich, full life

*God has given us all we need to live a rich, full life in Him.*

in Him. It's up to us to do the work that will enable us to have that kind of life. We need to be breaking up the hard ground of our hearts so that they can become tender and loving toward God and others. We need to sow the seeds of God's Word in our spirits so that we can stand on His promises through good days and bad. We must do the little things that matter the most—reading the Bible, praying, praising, worshipping, and fellowshipping with other believers. We must be responsible in putting on the armor of God.

> *Therefore take up the whole armor of God, that you may be able to withstand in the evil day, and having done all, to stand. Stand therefore, having girded your waist with truth, having put*

*on the breastplate of righteousness, and having shod your feet with the preparation of the gospel of peace; above all, taking the shield of faith with which you will be able to quench all the fiery darts of the wicked one. And take the helmet of salvation, and the sword of the Spirit, which is the word of God.* (Ephesians 6:13–17)

In this way, we can become men and women who are spiritually minded. We will be able to face times of adversity with hearts full of faith instead of giving in to our flesh and the negativity that Satan brings to us when we feel pain and anguish.

Guilt can be overcome, but it will take a committed effort on your part to stand strong in faith and continually fight against the condemning thoughts that Satan brings to your mind. *"Your adversary the devil walks about like a roaring lion, seeking whom he may devour. Resist him, steadfast in the faith"* (1 Peter 5:8–9).

# A Note from Cheryl for Caregivers Regarding Guilt

When Gabrielle became sick, Harry and I decided to take on the responsibility of becoming her caregivers. Our little girl was so young that we didn't want her to be frightened by the countless medical procedures she would have to endure. We wanted someone who was close to her and loved her to be there for her through the hard times. We had a faint notion of just how much was involved in being caregivers, but we never could have imagined the depth of heartache we would experience while caring for her.

I did almost all the daily, hands-on care for Gabrielle's needs. I bathed her, dressed her, and changed her medical dressing every five days. I drew her blood, took her blood pressure, and administered and regulated her medication twenty-four hours a day. Gabrielle had to take an incredible amount of pills every day. Before she became sick, she had never taken a pill in her life. After she became ill, though, she understood that taking pills was better than trying to take all her medicine in liquid form. So, within two weeks of her diagnosis, she was taking numerous pills each day. Gabrielle also had to drink an unbelievable amount of water each day.

It was almost more than I could bear to be the one who always told Gabrielle what she had to do just to live another day. I watched as she took pill after pill and drank more water than the rest of the family drank in a day. The steroids and IV medications she took ballooned her little body to nearly triple its original weight. I wasn't the only one who felt the enormous burden of this tragic sickness, either. Gabrielle, obviously, had to deal with it as none of us did. On very rare occasions, she would become irritated by everything she had to do. She would lash out at me for "making" her do all these things. I tried my best to let these outbursts go, as I knew she needed an outlet to let go of her anger and frustration. I knew it wasn't my precious Gabrielle talking. It was her weakened, hurting flesh that lashed out in those moments of anger and despair. Still, it hurt my heart to hear her during these times—not because of what she said, but because my daughter had to endure this.

Every so often, there came a time when it was just she and I in the room, and she would stare into my eyes. I could sense such a longing in her little eyes that it

touched me in the very core of my being. It was like she was trying to tell me, "Mommy, do something! Make it go away!" A few times, she verbalized this intense desire to have her normal life back. She would say, "Mommy, when can I play again? When can I swim again? When will all of this be over?"

It was in those quiet, tender moments when my broken heart would go out to her. She would lay her head on my shoulder and cry, her entire body shaking with each sob. These moments only lasted a few minutes, though, because someone would inevitably come in to the room and Gabrielle would immediately stop. She would never let anyone else see her in pain. She always made sure that everyone else saw the strong little trooper who would never give in or give up.

*I had to learn to find God in the quiet place of my spirit.*

In those rare instances when Gabrielle let the tears flow, I would hold her and comfort her. I would tell her that it was all going to be okay and that it would be over soon. I would smile and try to act happy in front of her, but, slowly, my heart was being crushed with the pain of seeing my little girl like this. It forced me to find a quiet place within myself where only God could find me and understand what I was going through.

I had always run to God before when my heart was broken. Each time, He healed me, and I returned to my life feeling whole once again. With Gabrielle, it was different. It was as if the heartache was never going to end. Daily, I had to learn to find God in the quiet place of

my spirit. It was the only place I could find peace in the midst of what seemed to be unbearable circumstances.

As her primary caregiver, I took on a lot of emotional baggage. In the beginning, it was easy to do what I needed to do for my daughter. I always had enough patience to do whatever Gabrielle wanted me to do, and I always had enough energy for her. I'd get up in the middle of the night anytime she wanted me to just sit with her. As the months went by, though, I found myself succumbing to the lack of sleep and the cancer in my own body that I didn't even know about yet. Eventually, I wouldn't even wake up when Gabrielle poked me in the middle of the night to get me up. These are the times that come back to haunt me, when I wish I could have done more for my daughter.

If I had known how it was all going to end, maybe I would have done things differently. Maybe I wouldn't have made Gabrielle do anything at all. Maybe I would have let her skip all the medications and the treatments that she had to endure. Maybe I wouldn't have subjected her to the steroids that swelled her little body so much that she eventually became self-conscious about her appearance.

It's so easy to look back and see what more I could have done, or to think about what I could have done differently. It's easy to feel guilty and even responsible for my little girl's passing. I still occasionally wrestle with thoughts like these. I keep coming back to the cross to lay them down and remind myself that it isn't about me. It has always been and will always be about God. I simply refuse to let these thoughts rule my life. I remember the words of Isaiah 43:18–19—*"Forget the former*

*things; do not dwell on the past. See, I am doing a new thing! Now it springs up; do you not perceive it? I am making a way in the desert and streams in the waste-land"* (NIV). I hold on to these prophetic words. God doesn't ever go back and try to fix my past, so why should I? Daily, I have to choose to have no regrets. I have to choose to let it go and find the quiet place where only God's peace rules.

If you have been or are a caregiver, please understand that you are a precious servant of God. He sees your sacrifice and your pain. He knows the love you have for the one you cared for or are now caring for. He doesn't want you to feel unappreciated, unloved, or guilty about anything. You have His approval for a job well done, and your reward in heaven will be great. Be encouraged, and don't give up the fight! You are a vital part of God's plan for your family and friends. Stay the course, and let God be God in every one of your circumstances until you one day hear Him say, *"Well done, good and faithful servant"* (Matthew 25:21).

*God doesn't ever go back and try to fix our pasts, so why should we?*

## *Points to Ponder*

1. a. What are some things you have felt or are feeling guilty about?

 

 

b. How have you dealt with feelings of guilt in the past?

 

 

2. What are some steps you can take to keep your mind focused on God's promise to give you every-thing you *"need for life and godliness"* (2 Peter 1:3 NIV) in the midst of problems that arise in your life?

## Chapter Nine

# *What Do You Say?:*

# *Dealing with People*

### *By Harry*

*I*was an executive with Oral Roberts Evangelistic Association for more than seventeen years. During that span, I spent a large portion of my time dealing with people. I found that, with the help of the Holy Spirit, the job came naturally to me. I was able to handle any situation that arose, no matter who it involved or the importance attached to it. After Gabrielle went home, I found myself having to deal with countless people who had something to say concerning her death, both in my private life and in my ministry. I discovered that dealing with these people was a new challenge, one that I didn't always feel so comfortable confronting.

People would offer their condolences and share a word of encouragement, and I would feel grateful.

143

The next minute, I was ready to fly off the handle because of some insensitive remark that someone had made about how we handled our daughter's situation. I quickly found out that it was a whole lot harder to deal with people when I failed to remain coolly objective and unemotional about the situation, as I had been able to do in many situations during my years as an executive. Now, I was emotionally charged and found it much harder to handle what people were saying to me. After all, it was my family that people were talking about.

If you have lost a loved one, you will also have to deal with the people who come to you and offer their support, words of healing, advice, or criticisms. There will be people who will love you to the last and do all they can to help you through the healing process. There will be people who love you and try their best to help, even though their "help" sometimes ends up making you feel worse. Sadly, there will also be people who have been just waiting for a chance to judge and criticize you for your "lack of faith" or "denial of reality."

The key to dealing with all of these people is the same: love. A heart of love will appreciate those who encourage us and lift us up with their kind and heartfelt words. A heart of love will understand and still be thankful when people who mean well say the wrong things. A heart of love will also help us turn the other cheek when someone has a bone to pick with us in the midst of our suffering. Is it easy to walk in love when people are critical and mean-spirited? Of course not. That doesn't change the fact that God wants us to keep walking in love. In fact, it is His commandment that we *"love one another"* (John 13:34).

We must be careful about the ways we react to people during our times of grief. As I already mentioned in a previous chapter, if we speak careless and hurtful words to those around us, we will feel the effects of those words in our relationships. God is big enough to keep your tongue from speaking reckless words that could cause people pain for years to come. He can protect you from doing something that may bring severe pain to others and, in turn, to yourself. Be open to His leading as He gives you wisdom on when to speak and when to hold your tongue.

## Be Ready

One thing that was difficult for Cheryl and me to handle was the fact that others were constantly reminding us of our daughter. In the beginning, it may have been because people wanted to help us (or hurt us, as the case may be). As time went on and we began to recover emotionally, people would still bring up Gabrielle's passing, perhaps out of respect or because they felt the need to do so. I remember once when Cheryl and I were Christmas shopping not long after Gabrielle went home. On a number of occasions, people who knew us would stop to talk to us about Gabrielle and her passing. We knew that these people were doing it out of love, but talking about our daughter opened up wounds that were still too raw to deal with then. We would break into tears each time we listened to these people talk about our little girl. It came so suddenly, as we were just walking around a mall and shopping, not even feeling depressed or sad. Then, bang! Out of the blue, our minds were pulled back to the sorrow and pain of the event.

These moments of being pulled back into the past even occurred while we were on the set taping

prerecorded television shows or shooting live programs. Sometimes, we were there because of our fight of faith for our daughter. However, other times, when we were there simply to minister, we would often end up discussing Gabrielle. It sometimes felt as though everyone wanted us to talk about it. At one point, I said to Cheryl, "I know we have some wonderful insights about grief to share with hurting people, but I don't want our family or our ministry to be centered or built on the home-going of our daughter. We must go on. We can help people in other areas, as well. We can't let this dominate our lives. We need to go on to the future for our family."

Even in private, Cheryl and I would find our conversations drifting to topics related to Gabrielle. All this added up, and we finally realized that we were letting it drag us down to a place of greater sorrow. We knew at that point that we had to make a decision about talking to each other and others about our daughter. We wanted to go forward and move on to the future.

We certainly are not saying that we wanted to forget our daughter. We will never forget her or the special place she had—and has—in our lives. What we are saying is that speaking too much about a departed loved one can move grieving people backward in the healing process. It can begin to dominate the minds of those who, of course, still miss the loved one who left. A good measuring stick for monitoring this is to consider what you speak about more—your departed loved one or the family you still have. For us, we took note of whether our conversations focused more on Gabrielle or on our two boys. Gabrielle will always be our daughter, but we began to recognize that our sons deserved and needed to be the topic of our conversations.

We also decided to make a conscious effort to change the subject if we found ourselves talking too much about Gabrielle. Again, we didn't mind talking about her. However, we simply did not want our conversations to be dominated by the past. For us, it would have been too much to handle. We were fighting against letting it dominate our private conversation because of the public nature of our ministry. Because we spoke with countless people face-to-face day after day, we would have never gotten off the subject if we hadn't decided to limit our conversation about Gabrielle in private.

When it came to dealing with those who brought up Gabrielle during conversation, we made a slightly different decision. We sat down as a family and discussed how we should handle these situations. After we all thought and talked about it, we decided that, when conversations with others drifted back to Gabrielle's home-going, we would talk freely about it and honor her memory. We also decided to try to move the conversation on to what we were doing in our lives today if we were able to. In this way, we figured we could minister to others who might be in need by allowing them to see how we handled adversity in our own lives.

So, in your efforts to respond to people in love, also keep in mind that you should think about what you're going to say and do ahead of time. For you, maybe it would be better if you decided that you are going to talk about it within your own family but limit discussion outside the house. Or, perhaps you would rather limit discussion of the topic no matter where you are. Whatever you decide, please remember that there is not one single approach that works for everyone. As long as your decision keeps your mind from being dominated by your

lost loved one, you can rest in the fact that you are on the road to complete healing and restoration.

## *Be Honest*

As I mentioned previously, when you are going through the mourning process, people are going to say things to you that hurt you and make you feel worse than you already do. If you are a person of faith, you will probably face this scenario more than those who are not believers. We found out that, when something tragic happens to people of faith, they become walking targets with "bull's-eyes" on their backs. We felt as if some people were just waiting for us to come into contact with them so that they could offer us their overly critical advice about what we should do as well as opinions about our faith as Christians. It was so obvious that some of these people wanted nothing more than to judge us, find fault with us, and even try to get us to back off our beliefs.

We received letters that asked us many unbelievable questions: "How can you, as people of faith, explain your failure?" "How could this happen to you?" "What is going to happen to your ministry now that your faith has failed?" To be sure, not all these questions were asked with a critical attitude. However, some of them certainly were, and we just couldn't believe that people could sit in the seat of judgment and say such stupid and hurtful things to us.

When you find yourself stuck in situations where people are saying things to you that cut you deeply, be honest with them. Tell them as lovingly as you can that, even though you are sure they are trying to help, their

words aren't coming across as they probably think they are. Explain to them that you're still feeling a lot of pain and that what they are saying is only making you feel worse. If these people are family members or friends who are genuinely concerned about you, they will most likely apologize and maybe even offer to help you in whatever way they can. If the person gets defensive with you or further criticizes you, it's time to walk away. Such people simply can't see that you are doing your best to move on toward the future and that you don't need to be pulled back into the past—into the place of more pain and anguish.

I call some of these hard-hearted people "professional mourners." In Bible times, and even in modern society, people actually made their livings by acting as mourners at funeral services. The only difference between those mourners and the people I call "professional mourners" is that the former got paid for their time and trouble. The people I call "professional mourners" are those who can't let go of their own past tragedies. They have lost loved ones of their own, and they refuse to let them go. They "carry" their loved ones wherever they go—either as memories that they always feel compelled to share or perhaps as photographs that they simply have to show you while you are trying to heal from your own grief. Three major signs will identify a "professional mourner." First, they are more concerned with telling you about their lost loved ones than they are with finding out how you are progressing in life after your own loss. Next, they insist on showing you photos or articles that remind them of their lost loved one when they come to visit you in your time of mourning. Last, these people will make remarks such as, "How can you be so callous as to go on a vacation, or celebrate Christmas, or go to

a party?" "How can you even think about selling your home and moving away?" "How can you even consider going on a date or getting remarried after you said good-bye to your spouse?" Sadly, people such as this are out there. You may run into them during your own time of mourning. Treat them with love, but realize that they don't have your best interests at heart. All they are thinking about is themselves and their own loss.

Remember that the key to dealing with people is love. If you are honest with them in a loving way and if they have your best interest in mind, they will under-stand. They may even tell you that they were just trying to help, but they didn't know what to say. Tell them that you appreciate their efforts and that you value their friendship.

*The key to dealing with people is love.*

## *Be Careful*

One other point I'd like to make here is that we need to be careful about the advice that people give us during our times of grief.

I recall one day when a young lady approached me and told me that her husband had been killed in an auto accident three months earlier. She said that she was only in her twenties and had three small children to raise by herself. As she talked to me, I could see the intense pain in her eyes. She then asked me when she should move on with life and how she should go about doing this. Knowing that her husband had passed on only a short time ago, I asked the young lady why she felt as though she had to be completely healed after

only three months. She appeared to be confused by my question and said that she had been given the impression that she should already be completely over her husband's death and ready to get on with her life. I was shocked. I asked who gave her such an idea. She replied that a particular woman in her church asked her on numerous occasions when she was going to get over her husband's death and when she was going to start living her life again.

I couldn't believe that someone had been insensitive enough to say such thoughtless things to this grieving young widow and mother. I looked at the young lady and said that there was no set timeline for the grieving process. I explained to her that everyone is different and moves through the process at his or her own rate of healing. I also made sure to encourage her that, as long as she was moving forward in life, God would help her through the process. Finally, I told her to pay no attention to what that insensitive and ignorant person had said to her.

She smiled and began to laugh about the whole thing. I could tell from her response that she had finally embraced the process with an honest and realistic perspective.

I was happy to have the chance to talk to this young lady and help her in her own grieving process. My heart goes out to those people who have listened to and heeded the ridiculous words of others in their efforts to process the pain that they are feeling. So, be very careful about how you act on what others say. Always let God be your guide. Pray that the Holy Spirit would help you discern what you have heard so that you can separate the choice

words from the empty ones. If you trust Him, He will guide you in the way. *"Trust in the LORD with all your heart, and lean not on your own understanding; in all your ways acknowledge Him, and He shall direct your paths"* (Proverbs 3:5–6).

# A Note from Cheryl Regarding What We Say to Children

Speaking in love certainly doesn't end with just those who are critical of us. We must make a conscious effort to speak in love to everyone around us, especially children who may be hurting and confused as they come to grips with their own grief. When Gabrielle went home to be with the Lord, we had to figure out what to tell children who had been her faithful friends and had prayed for her and with her during her sickness. In the beginning, the children weighed on my heart. I wanted to keep them from being hurt in any way. These children had become very close to our family, and, as a mother, I felt a special bond to these kids who were so selfless in their constant friendship to our daughter.

I remember one little boy, who was just six months older than Gabrielle. He would come over to the house, lay his hands on Gabrielle, and pray over her, believing absolutely that God would heal his friend. What would I say to him now that Gabrielle was in heaven?

One of Gabrielle's closest friends came over nearly every day just to be with her. Many times, Gabrielle asked if her friend could spend the night with us. Her precious little friend never minded; she always agreed to stay over.

Gabrielle's body was so swollen from her medications that it had nearly tripled in size during her sickness. Her friend never seemed to notice. When Gabrielle was unable to get down on the floor and play dolls anymore, her friend would sit with her on the bed, and they would color together. After a while, Gabrielle often could only play for a few minutes with her friend before she became so uncomfortable that she couldn't continue. Her friend didn't care. She would sit quietly by Gabrielle's bedside as if that was a perfectly normal way for five- and six-year-olds to spend time together. Toward the end, we would hear an occasional whisper or giggle come from Gabrielle's room when her friend was visiting, but even that slowly came to an end. But it never seemed to matter to her friend. She continued to come over as if it were a privilege to spend every moment she could with our sick daughter.

All of Gabrielle's friends put their faith on the line. They stood with us and believed with every fiber of their little beings that God was going to heal her.

The day after Gabrielle went home, Harry and I were getting ready for her home-going service when I had a complete emotional breakdown. "What are we going to tell the children?" I cried. I felt so guilty. I felt responsible for their tender hearts of faith and for their futures. I felt like screaming at myself for letting them take part in believing for Gabrielle's healing. I told myself that I was irresponsible and a complete idiot for allowing these children to put their faith on the line for Gabrielle's sake.

On the afternoon of the day that our daughter went to heaven, the mother of one of Gabrielle's friends called

and asked me if she could bring her daughters over for a moment. She said they needed to hear from me that everything was going to be okay. I said okay and then felt like dying as I waited for them to arrive. I cried out to God to give me something to say that wouldn't wound their little spirits.

After they arrived, I held the girls in my arms, not knowing what to say. All I could think as I held their precious little bodies in my arms was that I would never again hold my daughter on earth. We all began to cry, and the tears brought strength to each of us. Soon, I was telling the girls that everything was okay and that Gabrielle is alive and well. I said that Gabrielle just went to heaven ahead of us and that she would be waiting for us when we got there.

I felt so strongly that I needed to assure these girls that their friend was not dead and that none of us did anything wrong. Only later did I realize why I felt the need to say these things when I was so emotionally and physically overwhelmed—*I needed to hear these words myself.*

That afternoon meeting with the children helped me as much as it did them. At the home-going service the next day, my heart melted with joy when I saw so many children sitting in the service. Our sons were there along with nieces, nephews, and many of Gabrielle's friends. I put on a good face in front of everyone, but I knew if I had to say anything in front of everyone, I would crack. Harry, though, said he had something to say. I knew I couldn't do it, that, if I did, my emotions would erupt. I figured I could just stand next to Harry and let him address the crowd.

When our turn came to go up onto the platform, Harry took my arm and led me to the podium. I grabbed the podium and held on tightly, thinking that I could hold on if I stayed focused and didn't look anyone in the eyes. As Harry took the microphone and spoke, I looked out and saw the faces of children—some looked confused, and many of them looked as if they must have hurting little hearts. I took the microphone when Harry was through and started speaking. I didn't think about it. I didn't feel anything. I just began to speak.

I told everyone that Gabrielle carried a powerful anointing while she walked on this earth. As I spoke, it dawned on me that her anointing still remained on earth because she had no need for it in heaven. Immediately, I knew what my duty was in that moment of pain and confusion. I knew what the children needed to hear.

"Gabrielle's anointing did not go with her to heaven," I said. "She doesn't need it there. The anointing of the Holy Spirit stays on earth, so her anointing is still here. My job today is to transfer that anointing to you children who would like to have it in your lives so you can do what God has called you to do here on earth. If you want this anointing, then stand up!"

Our son Harry stood up immediately, and Roman, a timid and shy boy despite his incredible gifts and abilities, also jumped up from his seat as if he had been poked with a needle. It was as if Roman was saying, "I want it, and it's mine!" I knew that Roman would never be the same from that day on. I could just see it on his face. He took the anointing that day and ran with it. He became fearless in our ministry, and he began to do what he has been called to do with a holy boldness.

I was so thankful that the Lord gave me the words to say to the children that day. Many children wanted to have Gabrielle's anointing on their lives, and I know that God was able to minister healing to their wounded hearts and troubled souls on that special day.

When we discuss a loved one's departure with children, we need to be open, honest, and truthful with them in a loving and gentle way. We need to make clear the fact that none of us will ever live forever on this earth, and that a beautiful place called heaven awaits us if we believe.

Kids also need to understand that adults cry over loved ones because they love them and will miss them. It is by no means a sadness caused by thoughts of where they the loved one has now gone.

We must also be truthful in our actions. Children learn by example. You can tell them not to do something a hundred times, but they'll go right ahead and do it if they see you do it once. When there is incongruency between what we say and what we do, it can be confusing to kids. If we tell our children that we are okay and happy that our loved one is in heaven, but we are always sad and depressed, they will quickly pick up on it.

*We must be truthful in our actions.*

Guard your words, and watch your actions so that the children you are around don't learn to fear death and be saddened by it. Remember that part of training up children in the way they should go includes building their faith in God so that they can learn to live in

good times and bad. If we constantly tell our children that the world is a frightening place, they will come to fear it. If we tell them that everyone is out to get them in life, they will become untrusting. However, if we tell them that God is a good God, they will grow spiritually and learn how to handle problems and adversity with a spirit of faith and trust in God. *"Therefore be imitators of God as dear children"* (Ephesians 5:1).

# Points to Ponder

1.  a. What are some things that people have said to you in the past that have really hurt you?

    b. How did you handle these people?

2.  In what ways do you need God's help in dealing with other people? Write out your answer, and then ask God to give you guidance in these areas.

## Chapter Ten
# Balancing Act:

# Focusing on What You Still Have

### By Cheryl

After Gabrielle went home, in the midst of the most intense grief I had ever experienced, I heard God say to me, "Stop focusing on what you don't have or you will lose what you do have." The words hit me hard, and they seemed cruel to me. I had just lost my daughter, and now God was telling me to quit thinking about her! I couldn't believe that God could be so seemingly cruel in my time of pain, but I slowly began to understand that what He said to me was for the purpose of protecting our family.

Gabrielle was gone, yes, but I still had a wonderful husband and two incredible sons. My family wasn't gone, and I knew God was trying to tell me that I needed to remember that Harry and the boys needed me as

much as I needed them. They looked to me for love and support in our hour of sorrow just as I leaned on them in our time of grief. As much as I understood what God was saying to me about taking care of what I still had in life, I felt as though I didn't have anything left to give. After the eleven-month battle to save our daughter's life and her subsequent home-going, I was spent—emotionally and physically used up.

Then, if that wasn't enough, I found out about the cancer that had been ravaging my body. At that point, all I could think was that I would finally have peace. I would go home to be with my Father in heaven. I didn't care anymore. I had no energy and no will to live. I wanted out of the horrible nightmare that my life had become.

Thankfully, God was faithful. He helped me stay strong in my faith, and He raised me up from my sickbed so that I could once again come to appreciate and cherish the family that He had given me. From that point on, I began to focus on what God had spoken to me about not dwelling on Gabrielle's departure. Instead, I began to think about the family that still surrounded me, and I began to do all I could to be the best wife and mother that I could be.

## Count Your Blessings

After the loss of a loved one, it is easy for us to focus only on what we have lost. We hurt, and rightfully so—our lost loved ones leave an emptiness in our hearts that can only be healed by the Lord and His process of restoration. However, God did not ever mean for us to get so focused on what we no longer have that we lose sight of the other precious blessings He has given to us.

The family we still have is from God, and they need us. Our role as a spouse, parent, sibling, child, or other relative doesn't end. All of our family members were placed in our lives for a reason, and we need to be sensitive to their needs. In the midst of grief and sorrow, it's not easy. It's like a balancing act. On the one hand, you need to work through the mourning process, but, on the other hand, you also need to count the blessings that God has given you in the way of family and remain a vital part of the lives of those closest to you.

Perhaps, after your loss, you feel as though you no longer have family, and you don't see any blessings worth counting in life. Maybe you lost your spouse and none of your family lives near you. Well, what about friends? Your friends are still your friends even after your loss. They still need your friendship, and I am sure that, if you are grieving, you could still use their friendship as well.

Friends and family are just two of the blessings we can count while we are going through the healing process. Think of all the other earthly blessings that we can focus on in our pain: our churches, our communities, our pets, our favorite hobbies, and our jobs. Then, there are the wondrous blessings that come from above: our relationships with God, our salvation through Christ, the friendship of the Holy Spirit, the Bible, and the magnificence of God's marvelous creation. I am sure there are other things we could count as blessings, too, if we thought about it. The point is that there is always something to focus on and give thanks to God for. There is always something to pour our lives into if we look hard enough. As I said, it's a balancing act. We need to maintain steady progress in the healing process and, at the

same time, remain life-giving and thankful children of God. So, don't get stuck focusing on what you no longer have in your life. Instead, go forward, and live a life that enjoys and appreciates the blessings of God that you still have. Life is meant to be lived today and then day by day. *"Do not remember the former things, nor consider the things of old. Behold, I will do a new thing, now it shall spring forth"* (Isaiah 43:18–19). Keep your eyes on what you have and the wonderful future that God has in store for you.

## The Family Still Remains

*Keep your eyes on the wonderful future that God has in store for you.*

When a loved one goes home to be with the Lord, it affects every family member differently, and it also has the potential to throw the family out of balance. A family is somewhat like a mobile: It hangs together in perfect balance. When one piece is removed from a mobile, its balance is thrown off and it hangs in disorder. The same thing can happen to a family who has lost one of its members.

Before Gabrielle departed for heaven, each member of our family felt secure and safe in the family. Each of us knew his or her place, and we all functioned together in balance and harmony. We were very open and honest with each other. We felt complete and satisfied as a family unit. Then, Gabrielle left us. The pain in our hearts hindered the words that once came so easily. The sorrow we each felt weighed us down emotionally. The

grief that welled up in our souls threw us out of balance. We truly were like a mobile that had lost one of its pieces, and we needed to learn how to be a family again. We needed to learn how to bring balance back to our family even though one of our members was gone. We knew we would never truly bring our family to a state of "completeness" because we understood that Gabrielle had become a part of our future. Therefore, we focused on going on with our lives together, as the family that God has called us to be.

Bringing our family back into balance took an effort on our part. We all needed to process the grief in our lives while also going on with life as a wife/mother, husband/father, and son/brother. Harry and I were barely hanging on emotionally as we tried not only to help our own family, but also to continue to minister to others. Identifying and acting on the needs of our family wasn't easy for us. At first, we weren't even able to recognize some of the needs within the family, specifically with our two boys. It didn't seem to us that anything was too out of the ordinary with them, but, as the months went on, we began to find out that Roman and Harry had some serious issues they were struggling with. We were in such pain that we didn't even notice how much our sons needed us. Thankfully, God remained faithful and turned our attention to the needs of our sons.

When a family goes through a crisis, children discover that the people they always relied on are in a desperate state. Parents are fighting the grief that is in their hearts, and their children are watching them, knowing that something isn't right. The support system for children often fails because parents forget

that their children still need them in the same ways they did before the tragedy, as well as needing them for additional support in the time of grief. Not only do parents sometimes forget about their children's needs, but they also are often so focused on their own sorrow and how to deal with it that they do things that may be incredibly painful for their children.

Right after Gabrielle went home to be with the Lord, Harry told our sons, "Don't talk to Mom about Gabrielle yet. It hurts her too much." As we related earlier, we also took down every photograph of Gabrielle, as well as all her artwork. For Harry and me, this was a way to cope with the grief we felt. We also began doing things that the boys did not understand. For example, we avoided doing things that reminded us of Gabrielle and her absence. We avoided setting the table because there was always a plate missing. We didn't buy three-packs of candy bars for the boys because there now would be one remaining.

Through all this, Roman and young Harry didn't say anything about how they felt. They pushed down their emotions because they wanted to appear strong for Mom and Dad. Young Harry didn't even appear to miss Gabrielle, acting as though he was oblivious to the whole process of grieving. He would often console me and hug me, saying, "It will be okay, Mom." Roman didn't seem sure how to react. Every so often, he would say, "I know Gabrielle isn't here, but is it okay if I think about her?" Can you imagine the pain that must have been in his little heart to have uttered words such as these?

Finally, Harry and I found out how badly our boys needed us and how far we had fallen short in meeting

their needs. In mid-summer of 2000, less than a year after Gabrielle had gone home, we were working on a ministry message titled, "What's in the Box?" It was based on an episode of *The Andy Griffith Show* called "Mayberry Goes Bankrupt." In the episode, an old man in Mayberry had nothing left to pay his bills, and Andy was forced to evict him from his house. While Andy was in his house, ready to evict him, the man produced a box, hoping it contained something of value to help his cause. In the box, the man found a whale bone, a decorative collector's spoon, and an old worthless bond.

Any of us would probably laugh at what the man found in his box, but he kept those items because they reminded him of special moments in his life. With that in mind, Harry and I decided to write a message that asked people the question, "What's in the Box?" of their lives. While we were working on this message, Harry opened up young Harry's strongbox and found a wallet, some money, a letter from his grandma, and pictures of Gabrielle. I opened up Roman's box and found his wallet and pictures of Gabrielle.

Harry sat the boys down and asked, "Okay, guys, what's going on here?" They responded, "We can't forget our sister!"

It hit us so hard then that everything we had been doing to deal with our grief had made it harder for the boys to deal with theirs. Roman and Harry had taken all our words and actions to mean that the entire family had to forget Gabrielle completely. In the months that followed, we became more sensitive to the needs of our sons. At one point, young Harry said he didn't want to

travel and minister anymore, and he seemed upset at everyone and everything.

We asked him, "Harry, why don't you want to travel?"

"I just want to stay home awhile," he responded.

In our minds, we understood that home was where he could feel as though he was closer to Gabrielle. So, we probed further.

"What is really bothering you?" Harry asked our son.

"Mama gets mad at me. You get mad at me. I can't even talk about Gabrielle!"

"I didn't know you wanted to talk about Gabrielle," Harry said.

"I miss her," young Harry said. "I miss going in and playing with her. I miss listening to her sing while I'm sitting in her room. I miss buying her new dolls and opening them."

"You need to talk about it?" Harry asked.

"Yes."

"It's fine to talk about it," Harry said. "Mama and I can handle it."

For the next thirty minutes, we sat and listened as young Harry poured out his heart and vented his emotions.

Harry and I had been stifling our sons' emotions to dangerous levels. So, when we knew that our boys

needed to talk about and remember Gabrielle, we made a conscious effort to help them do it. When we were at church one night, young Harry asked me, "I wonder what Gabrielle is doing right now?"

"I don't know," I said. "What do you think?"

"Well," he said, "if she were here with us, she would probably be calling Roman over to the drinking fountain and trying to stick his head under the water. She just loved picking on Roman!"

Roman, on the other hand, began to talk about what Gabrielle was probably doing up heaven. Once, he said to his father, "You know, Dad, Gabrielle's up there with her big water gun playing with Grandpa and Gran Gran."

We, too, began to shift our focus in regard to speaking about our daughter. At first, all we talked about was the tragic story of how she had died. However, we instead started to speak about how she lived and the fact that she is still living. Our boys helped pull us away from the sickbed Gabrielle departed from and move us to the here and now, where our daughter is alive and well in heaven.

If you have a family, or even close friends, don't forget that they still are a part of your life. How you react to grief will affect them and your relationships with them. Make a conscious effort to stay sensitive to their needs and feelings so that, as you try to progress in the healing process, you won't create further pain for those closest to you. When you feel emotionally secure enough to do so, do things together that you used to do. Go places that you used to go. Pray together, and spend

time together talking about the things of God. Friends and family members will heal at their own rate, and so will you. So, do what you can to keep those closest to you close to you.

## *Open Up*

One way to make sure that you maintain balanced relationships with those closest to you is to be open with

*Be open with friends and family—they aren't mind readers.*

them. Your family and friends aren't mind readers. They won't always know how you are feeling or why you did something that you did. Instead of suppressing your emotions, tell those closest to you how you are feeling. You may say to a spouse, "I'm really down right now. I feel out of control. Don't worry, though. It's not you, and it won't last. So, if you hear me screaming at the mirror, you'll know what's going on!"

Sometimes, we mistakenly think that our loved ones should know what we are thinking and feeling without us even telling them. We may say to ourselves, "If they really loved me, they would know what's wrong." However, your loved ones can't possibly know exactly how you are feeling all the time. In fact, if you are going through a particularly tough time and you don't express your emotions, your loved ones will more than likely think the worst—things like, "Boy, Mom must be mad at me" or "What is wrong with her today!" If our loved ones don't understand what we are feeling, they will have to guess, and they will probably guess wrong.

Conversely, we need to be ready to help our loved ones express the emotions they are feeling. Sometimes, loved ones may be afraid or intimidated to share what is heavy on their hearts. I will never forget the first time that Roman got sick after his sister had gone to heaven. He was in bed and seemed nervous. We checked on him every few minutes, even though we knew he would probably be over it in a few hours. At one point, we peeked around the door, and Roman had the strangest look on his face. We walked into his room and sat on the edge of his bed.

We asked him, "Son, are you okay?"

He looked up at us with eyes that were more serious than we had ever seen them.

"Mommy and Daddy," he said, "am I going to die?"

We felt so bad for him! Being just a young boy, he didn't understand the difference between a minor virus and the disease that Gabrielle had. All he knew was that one day his sister was okay, then she was sick, and, finally, she went to heaven. If we hadn't done the simple little task of asking our son what was wrong, he would have stayed in bed that night, wide awake with fear and worry.

One way to make sure loved ones feel comfortable sharing their hearts with you, and with each other, is to agree ahead of time that anyone can open up at any time and say anything without fear of consequences. Children especially need to know that parents aren't going to get mad about something they say. If everyone knows that they can be open and honest, it will help bring the family back together and into harmony.

Perhaps some of your loved ones are more introverted, and it takes a lot to get them to open up. This is a situation where you can think of questions that may spur them to open up and express their emotions, thus helping them along in the healing process and also helping to solidify the family unity. Put some thought into such questions. Your list should be individually tailored to the person you have in mind. When you think about these questions, please remember that they should be open-ended to avoid getting simple "yes" or "no" answers. Also, make sure the questions can't possibly be taken as critical or mean-spirited. Remember that the person you are trying to help is also hurting. They need to hear positive words of affirmation and love.

Here are a few questions that may help you in this process:

- "I miss doing things now that (name) isn't here with us. What do you miss doing with him/her?"

- "What do you think (name) would want us to do now that he/she isn't here with us anymore?"

- "What are some of the best memories you have of spending time with (name)?"

- "What do you remember about (name) that you never want to forget?"

These are just a few sample questions that you may be able to use. I am sure that, with some thought, you will think of others that will help your loved ones deal with their grief.

Also, make a point of spending quality time on an individual basis with those closest to you. If you're a wife, make sure you give your husband some quiet time that you can spend going for a drive or eating out. If you're a parent, be there for your kids and do things with them one-on-one that help them get back to living life. These private times with loved ones give us a chance to take their emotional "temperatures" and gauge where they are in the healing process. It also helps build the bond between family members (or close friends).

## Do What It Takes

Remember: Life is going to go on whether you decide to or not. The people around you are also going to go on with life. How you handle your grief is not only going to affect you, but it is also going to play a vital role in how those closest to you process their own grief. Make it a point to keep a godly attitude throughout the mourning process. Don't get stuck focusing on what you don't have. Learn to see the blessings of God all around you, and do what you can to enrich the lives of your loved ones. As I've said throughout this chapter, when you keep the right attitude and progress through the healing process in a healthy way, you are not just helping yourself; you are also helping those around you who are going through the same process. Your willingness to go on with life will help bring your relationships back into harmony and balance so that you and those you love will move from grief to glory together! *"Two are better than one, because they have a good reward for their labor"* (Ecclesiastes 4:9).

## *Points to Ponder*

1. Psalm 103:2 says *"Praise the LORD, O my soul, and forget not all his benefits"* (NIV). List all the blessings of God in your life that you can think of in the next five minutes.

## Chapter Eleven

# *Dreaming of Heaven:*

# Keeping an Eternal Perspective

### *By Cheryl*

For a Christian, heaven takes on a new meaning when you have a child who lives there. Before you say good-bye to a child or to any of your loved ones, heaven is a place you probably believe in with all your heart. However, after your loved one departs from this world and goes to a great reward with the Lord, heaven becomes a real, physical place in your mind. In your heart and in your head, you *know* there is a heaven where your loved one is dancing and singing the praises of the Lord in the shadow of His wings.

For me, heaven became an even more wonderful reality after Gabrielle went home. I knew without a doubt that our little girl was with her heavenly Father, free from any pain or tears and completely healed. I

wanted more, though. I wanted to be able to picture in my mind exactly what it is like for Gabrielle to live the rest of her days in heaven. I knew and loved everything that the Bible has to say about heaven, but I cried out in prayer for the Lord to show me more. The Lord answered my prayer by speaking to me through a dream—a dream that helped me through the process of healing and restoration.

## A Dream Like No Other

One night, after I had prayed to the Lord for greater revelation regarding our daughter's being in heaven, I dreamed a dream like none that I had ever had. In the dream, which was more like a vision that I was actually a part of, I found myself in heaven. Gabrielle was there, as well. She was in a room that seemed to be some sort of school. The schoolroom, standing alone in a meadow surrounded by mountains, was magnificent, with dark-stained, decoratively carved wood walls. In the center of the room, steps led down to an area lower than the rest of the room. It was in this area that Gabrielle was standing among a group of other children. There were many boys and girls, and they appeared to represent many different nations from around the world. Overseeing the children were two beautiful, sweet women who wore glorious suits of clothes. The fabric of their clothing was like nothing I had ever seen on earth. Throughout the fabric, threading made of gold and silver was intricately woven. The fabric itself fit the women so well that it was as if the cloth was a part of their very being.

The children's clothing was equally magnificent. Each outfit was unique in its design and appearance.

The girls wore exquisite dresses of many vibrant colors. Gabrielle wore a gorgeous dress fitted to the waist with a flowing circular skirt. As with the overseers' clothing, Gabrielle's dress seemed to be a part of her. It was nearly formfitting, without any sign of it binding her anywhere. The little boys wore suits of deeply hued colors. It actually seemed that the fabric of the boys' suits was made up of more than one color. From different angles, the suits changed color. I could see shades of purples, reds, greens, and many other colors.

All through the room, knowledge bolted through the air like lightning. It wasn't spoken by anyone, but rather just shot back and forth throughout the room. I could see the "lightning" actually go into the children as they took in the knowledge. The children would absorb the knowledge and show their delight, sometimes touching each other and passing on the knowledge.

At one point, I tried to get Gabrielle to come with me. I longed for her to come back to earth with me. When I tried to get her attention, she didn't acknowledge me. She didn't actually ignore me, but she remained focused on learning more. It was then that I snapped out of the dream and woke up startled. I was excited because I had seen our daughter in heaven, but I was frustrated that I was unable to bring her home with me.

I went back to sleep, and I was immediately transported back to the heavenly vision of the schoolroom I had seen. As before, Gabrielle and the rest of the children were there, but the room was different. I'm not sure if it was a completely different room, or if it just evolved. Instead of richly ornamented wood, the walls were made of some sort of glasslike transparent material. Steps still

led down to an area in the center of the room, and the children were still receiving knowledge in the form of flashes of lightning. The children seemed so delighted and excited about being there and learning.

I felt as though I were outside, even though I was inside the schoolroom. I could see and feel bright, warm light, which was like the sun. I could see, feel, and smell the flowers and the grass. A breeze was blowing, and the children continued to learn at a speed beyond earthly comprehension. They were laughing, talking, and joyously participating in their learning experience. Once more, I tried to coax Gabrielle to come back home with me, but she didn't acknowledge or respond to me in any way.

*Our own selfish wants and desires may get in the way of what God wants to share with us.*

As before, I awoke with a start. I fell right back to sleep and rejoined Gabrielle in heaven. Once more, I was watching the children learn. I sensed that the air itself was completely charged with the knowledge that was being taught and learned. The knowledge was everywhere, permeating everyone and everything I could see. However, it wasn't permeating me. I was so focused on getting Gabrielle to come with me that I missed out on the incredible knowledge that flowed around me.

Looking back, I can see how this experience teaches a valuable lesson to us all. I now consider how our frame of mind affects what God is able to give us. God may be talking to us and teaching us—trying to help

us grow—but if we are too absorbed with other things, we may miss out. Our own selfish wants and desires may get in the way of what God wants to share with us. If we are not sensitive to the voice of God, we will not hear the sweet whisper of His words to us—we'll miss the chance to spend time with Him in the secret place of His love. If we are to plumb the depths of our relationships with God, we need to get close to Him and shed the worries and wants that weigh us down. We need to meditate on what He speaks to us, instead of immediately asking for more revelation. If we immerse ourselves in what He has already spoken to us, we will find so much knowledge and inspiration for our lives that we will feel beyond blessed!

If only I would have been focused on God's pure knowledge rather than my own intense desire to see Gabrielle return home with me. Thankfully, the dream continued. The children were still in the center area of a classroom, but, this time, the walls were made of flowers. Thousands of flowers were pressed into the form of the walls that enclosed the room. I could see through the flowers, smell the flowers, and even touch and pick

*If we are not sensitive to the voice of God, we will not hear the sweet whisper of His words to us.*

them. The flowers were alive, and, even after I picked one, it did not die. Nothing in heaven can die, for it is a place of life!

At some point—I have no idea when because time is irrelevant in heaven—I tried to get Gabrielle to come with me again. I simply thought about it without speaking, and it seemed as if the desire was conveyed as a

spoken request. Don't get me wrong: Words are spoken in heaven—words of praise, worship, and joy. In heaven, thoughts are also "spoken" as words, and my desire to have Gabrielle come with me was immediately known. Yet, again, she did not acknowledge me. She simply kept learning with the other children. I also took note of a little boy who had been next to her in the schoolroom in each of the visions. For some reason, I became more aware of the boy's presence. I even seemed to know the boy, but I couldn't understand who he might be.

For many days and months after that night of heavenly visions, I couldn't figure out who the little boy was. The Holy Spirit kept telling me, "You know this boy." However, I could not think of who the boy might be. Finally, as I continued to think about the little boy and ask the Lord to reveal his identity, it came to me. The boy in my dream was our little boy who went to heaven when I miscarried just months before Gabrielle was conceived. Our son Malachi is in heaven learning and growing with Gabrielle! That thought has brought me so much comfort since I finally understood that the boy in my visions was our son.

However, while I was having my vision, I couldn't comprehend the fact that the little boy was Malachi. I watched as he and Gabrielle continued to play. At one point, Gabrielle said something to him, and she used the word "them" when she should have used "those." I was so used to correcting my children's grammar after years of home-schooling that I automatically recognized the mistake in my mind. For the first time, Gabrielle turned toward me and acknowledged me. She looked at me with her piercing blue eyes and a countenance that sparkled with her sweetness. At the same time, though,

she exuded a strength and an understanding. She said, "The spot and wrinkle on the body of Christ are not those who need correcting. The spot and the wrinkle on the body of Christ are those who do the correcting."

Suddenly, I was awake again and emotionally shaken. I was sweating all over. I thought about the two sentences Gabrielle had spoken to me in my dream. I wasn't sure what she meant or for whom it was spoken. I went over her words again and again in my head until it finally hit me. Gabrielle was giving me a message from God Himself. I knew without a doubt that God was speaking to me through Gabrielle. But, what was He trying to tell me, and was the message about me?

## *Things Above*

I began to contemplate Gabrielle's message and what it meant. I wondered if pointing out Gabrielle's gram-matical mistake was judgmental in God's eyes. Was I too critical? I began to rationalize that I was simply doing what I had always done when trying to teach my children how to speak correctly. I certainly didn't want to be viewed by God as judgmental, critical, or even "correcting" because of what I thought about Gabrielle's mistake. I didn't want to admit, even to myself, that I was the one to whom Gabrielle's message was directed. But, then, my hard heart began to melt. I opened the veil that covered my rebellious spirit and stared at the reality of what was inside me—sin. Underneath the pride I wore as a pretty coat was my shameful weakness and sin. I cried out to God, "Lord, help me! Help me see who I really am. Help me not to be correcting, critical, and judgmental of others. Help me, Lord, to lead others,

to persuade others, to love others, but not to judge or criticize others. Help me to see my own weaknesses, shortcomings, and sin."

I knew I was guilty as charged of sitting in the seat of judgment. I knew that I had buried that horrible part of my personality so deep in my mind that I never thought about it or dealt with it as I should have. I began to cry, "Lord, help me have your perspective! Help me see situations and people through your eyes, not my own. Help me to be different, Lord!"

That day and the next few days, I continued to cry out to the Lord from my heart. Slowly, I processed the revelation of what was spoken to me. The Holy Spirit began to speak to my heart. He said that the Father is not looking for "sheriffs" to police the body of Christ. He reminded me that Jesus said, *"Go into all the world and preach the gospel to every creature"* (Mark 16:15). He didn't say to "shoot" people where they stand by judging and correcting them.

This whole chain of events also teaches us the important lesson of seeing things as God sees them. It's as Paul said in 2 Corinthians 5:7: *"For we walk by faith, not by sight."* I was seeing everyone through my own critical and judgmental eyes when I should have been looking at people through the eyes of faith and viewing people as God does. My view of reality was not a healthy one, and it apparently took the grieving process to bring this fact to light. Looking back, I am sure that learning this fact about myself helped me to stay on the road to complete restoration and recovery.

What about you? Are you looking at things from your own perspective? Do you have some weakness or

sin that "colors" how you see the people around you? Have you become so focused on your own pain and loss that it has become a selfish escape from life? It's time for believers to view their world through eyes of faith that see the best in every person and in every situation. I've heard it said that we sometimes get so heavenly minded that we're no earthly good. But, living the opposite way is much more dangerous, especially when you are dealing with the loss of a loved one. We must not be so earthly minded that we are no heavenly good.

Being able to keep a heavenly perspective while living on earth is not always easy. It is a continual process in which we must go deeper into the things of God and allow the Holy Spirit to reveal Himself to us little by little. Gaining a greater knowledge and understanding of God is a "layer-by-layer" process—the revelation of God we have right now must be understood and processed before we can experience and comprehend the next "layer" of who He is. So, stay close to God, grow in your knowledge

*We must not be so earthly minded that we are no heavenly good.*

and love of Him, and learn to look at your life and circumstances through His eyes—eyes that see you healed and whole, eyes that look at your wonderful future, eyes that see *"things which do not exist as though they did"* (Romans 4:17).

## *Points to Ponder*

1.  What are some Scriptures from the Appendix that could help you keep a more heavenly perspective in life? List three of them here, and commit them to memory.

    •

    •

    •

2.  Looking back over your past, how have you seen God continue to give you a deeper revelation of Himself?

## Chapter Twelve
# Bound for a Better Place:

## Recalling the Reward
## That Awaits

### By Harry

A s Cheryl mentioned in the last chapter, it is easy for Christians to believe in heaven in their minds. However, it seems that, many times, believers think of heaven as some far-off place that lacks substance or any physical attributes. While they may consent to the fact that heaven does exist, these people simply don't think of heaven in "real" terms. The Bible tells a different story. It describes heaven in vivid detail as the place that God has prepared for those who choose to live for Him during their lives on earth.

The reality of heaven hit me after Gabrielle went home to be with the Lord. At that point, I began to start think-

ing about heaven from a new perspective. I've told many people since then that you're confident that heaven is a real place when you have someone who lives there! Knowing that our daughter is alive and well in heaven gives heaven a "real" feeling in my mind and spirit.

Of course, Satan would much rather have us think about heaven in some sort of abstract way, as though it was some wished-for place we dream about. It's just one more way he can keep us shackled in our grief. He brings thoughts to our minds that tell us that heaven is not real and that we are foolish to believe in such a wonderful place. If we allow these thoughts to dominate our minds, we will quickly find ourselves despairing and fearing what happened to our lost loved ones. Thankfully, we don't need to be afraid about whether or not heaven exists, or even about what it may be like.

## *The Reality of Heaven*

In the Bible, Jesus spoke about heaven in the simplest of terms, leaving no doubt in His listeners' minds that He believed in a real place called heaven. It was not a conjured up place to ease the minds of men when they face death. No, to Jesus, heaven was as real as real could be. In John 14:1–3, Jesus said,

> *Do not let your hearts be troubled. Trust in God; trust also in me. In my Father's house are many rooms; if it were not so, I would have told you. I am going there to prepare a place for you. And if I go and prepare a place for you, I will come back and take you to be with me that you also may be where I am.* (NIV)

Does that sound like a man speaking about some dream world? I don't think so. Jesus understood the reality of heaven better than anyone. After all, He had come from heaven to earth. He knew all about the incredible magnificence that awaited those who would follow Him. Look at the description of heaven that the apostle John gave us in Revelation 21:10–26:

*And he carried me away in the Spirit to a great and high mountain, and showed me the great city, the holy Jerusalem, descending out of heaven from God, having the glory of God. Her light was like a most precious stone, like a jasper stone, clear as crystal. Also she had a great and high wall with twelve gates, and twelve angels at the gates, and names written on them, which are the names of the twelve tribes of the children of Israel: three gates on the east, three gates on the north, three gates on the south, and three gates on the west. Now the wall of the city had twelve foundations, and on them were the names of the twelve apostles of the Lamb. And he who talked with me had a gold reed to measure the city, its gates, and its wall. The city is laid out as a square; its length is as great as its breadth. And he measured the city with the reed: twelve thousand furlongs. Its length, breadth, and height are equal. Then he measured its wall: one hundred and forty-four cubits, according to the measure of a man, that is, of an angel. The construction of its wall was*

*Jesus understood the reality of heaven better than anyone.*

*of jasper; and the city was pure gold, like clear glass. The foundations of the wall of the city were adorned with all kinds of precious stones: the first foundation was jasper, the second sapphire, the third chalcedony, the fourth emerald, the fifth sardonyx, the sixth sardius, the seventh chryso-lite, the eighth beryl, the ninth topaz, the tenth chrysoprase, the eleventh jacinth, and the twelfth amethyst. The twelve gates were twelve pearls: each individual gate was of one pearl. And the street of the city was pure gold, like transparent glass. But I saw no temple in it, for the Lord God Almighty and the Lamb are its temple. The city had no need of the sun or of the moon to shine in it, for the glory of God illuminated it. The Lamb is its light. And the nations of those who are saved shall walk in its light, and the kings of the earth bring their glory and honor into it. Its gates shall not be shut at all by day (there shall be no night there). And they shall bring the glory and the honor of the nations into it.*

John continued this beautiful description of the reward that awaits us in Revelation 22:1–5:

*And he showed me a pure river of water of life, clear as crystal, proceeding from the throne of God and of the Lamb. In the middle of its street, and on either side of the river, was the tree of life, which bore twelve fruits, each tree yielding its fruit every month. The leaves of the tree were for the healing of the nations. And there shall be no more curse, but the throne of God and of the Lamb shall be in it, and His servants shall serve*

*Him. They shall see His face, and His name shall be on their foreheads. There shall be no night there: They need no lamp nor light of the sun, for the Lord God gives them light. And they shall reign forever and ever.*

Can you imagine what heaven is like? It is so majestic and awesome in its splendor that our finite minds can grasp it on only a small scale. I think it's safe to say that heaven is the most incredible thing we can imagine with our earthly minds— multiplied by trillions! God loves us so much that He has prepared this wonderful place for us to spend the rest of eternity with Him. This fact should keep our hearts full of hope, even in the midst of grief. We should do the work that God gives us to do in the here and now, all the while keeping an eye toward the glorious future that awaits us.

*Heaven is so majestic and awesome in splendor that our finite minds can grasp it on only a small scale.*

## Longing for a Better Place

Christians should long for heaven. We should always be looking forward to it. If we were able to grasp what awaits us in heaven, we'd be anxious to finally get "home." After all, the earth is not our home. In the Bible, Peter called us *"aliens and strangers in the world"* (1 Peter 2:11 NIV). Paul also spoke about this when he said that *"our citizenship is in heaven"* (Philippians 3:20). We need to keep in mind that we are bound for a better place. We are only traveling through the earth. This

means that we should be doing all we can to prepare ourselves for our true home and country. Too often, we spend incredible amounts of time and energy on living and planning our earthly lives, and we forget that we have another home that we should be thinking about. Remember what Hebrews 11:16 says about the saints of old: *"They were longing for a better country   a heavenly one"* (NIV).

If you are going through the grieving process, please keep in mind that we are not home yet. Allow the thought of what awaits us in heaven to give you comfort and joy while you are still here on earth. Make a decision to enjoy the life you have in the here and now, all the while eagerly anticipating your rich reward in eternity. Heaven will be such a wonderful place for us. Our struggles will be over. Our tears will be no more. We will see loved ones again. We will see Jesus face-to-face and spend eternity in the presence of God. This is our reward for a life lived for the Lord. It is such a glorious thing to think about that we should all remember to keep our focus on our true home. *"If then you were raised with Christ, seek those things which are above, where Christ is, sitting at the right hand of God. Set your mind on things above, not on things on the earth"* (Colossians 3:1–2).

## *Points to Ponder*

1. Based on the Scriptures about heaven found in the Appendix, what do you think heaven will be like?

2. a. Colossians 3:2 tells us to set our minds *"on things above, not on things on the earth."* What are some prevalent thoughts that keep your mind focused on earthly things?

   b. What are some steps you can take in learning to focus your mind on *"things above"* (such as God's love, mercy, grace, and His promises to you)?

## Chapter Thirteen
# Promise of a New Day:

# Choosing to Live Again

### By Harry and Cheryl

For a little more than three years after Gabrielle's passing, we journeyed on the difficult road of restoration and healing. We had our ups, and we certainly had our downs, as well. There were days when our faith was strong and overflowing, and then there were days when we felt as though we'd hit rock bottom. We've both had personal struggles to deal with, and our sons have had their own issues to work through. Through it all, though, we had each other. More than that, we had God leading us every step of the way. Even when we were at our wits' end and we lashed out at God in anger, He was there for us, as a loving Father who understood what we were feeling. His faithfulness

helped bring us through the process, and, today, we are enjoying the promise.

Do we still have hard days? Of course. Do we sometimes break down and cry? Absolutely. However, life goes on for us, and we are going on with it. We know that recovery is here at last. We believe that we have been healed and restored. You may ask, "What about your daughter?" We have the strong assurance in our hearts that she is still alive and well, just not here with us on earth. We have broken free from the crippling idea that she is part of our past. Instead, we know that she is in our future. Someday, we will be reunited with her when we all stand before Jesus in heaven.

## *Focusing on Life*

Even though it's been more than three years since our daughter went home to heaven, we consider ourselves to be just emerging from the grieving process. Because of the public nature of our ministry, we found ourselves constantly answering people's questions about our daughter and how to handle grief. In some ways, it helped us process our own grief by forcing us to deal with the issues at hand. However, perhaps it also lengthened the restoration process for us by keeping our daughter's passing at the forefront of our minds so often. Whatever the case may be, everything worked together for God's greater good, and we now are able to minister to others from a place of healing and understanding.

When we said good-bye to our daughter on this earth, we knew the journey toward recovery would be a long one. We had read statistics that said a majority of

couples who have lost a child end up divorcing. We knew the ramifications of our daughter's passing—our very family was at stake. We understood that the incredible pain and anguish that we were feeling was able to tear us apart. However, we made a decision that grief was not going to destroy our family. We set out on our mournful journey intent on handling our grief in the healthiest ways possible. We were determined to go through the process and embrace the promise with our faith not only intact, but stronger than ever.

As we've said throughout this book, it wasn't easy. Grief never is. As we just related, our public ministry added a new challenge for us in regard to the mourning process. We found ourselves trying to keep our own lives on track while also attempting to handle mountains of mail, numerous phone calls, and countless one-on-one questions—all from people who wanted to know how we

*The key is to focus on life.*

were going to handle this crisis. Many of these people knew about Gabrielle because her story had been shown on international television and told in churches around the world throughout the eleven months that she had battled the cancer in her body. Because of our profession of faith as believers, we were in a very vulnerable spot after our daughter went home. On the one hand, we faced the critics who pointed their fingers and said, "You must not have had enough faith, or else your daughter would have been healed!" On the other hand, we became almost instant "authorities" on grief and how to handle it.

Everyone who says good-bye to a loved one will have to deal with many issues, emotions, and people who

want to help or hurt them. The key is to focus on life. We chose each day to live above the sadness we felt. We took to heart the words of Paul in Philippians 3:14: *"I press on toward the goal to win the prize for which God has called me heavenward in Christ Jesus"* (NIV). We still live this way, pressing on toward the promises of God. We know that the word *press* implies that we are going to have to exert ourselves in our lives if we are to endure the process and embrace the promise. Jesus promised us all that we would have tough times in life, but He also promised that He would take care of us through them all: *"In the world you will have tribulation; but be of good cheer, I have overcome the world"* (John 16:33).

Jesus' command to *"be of good cheer"* is not always an easy one. It takes a conscious effort on our parts to focus on the life and blessings that God has given us. Jesus didn't say we had to be hilariously happy every second of the day. He did say, however, that we are to *"be of good cheer."* That means we should live lives that seek to find the good even in the midst of trials. We find ourselves appreciating things in life that we once would have taken for granted. Our decision to focus on the good and be cheerful has helped open our eyes to all the wonderful things around us. We gaze at the

*We should live lives that seek to find the good even in the midst of trials.*

snowcapped majesty of jagged mountain peaks and stand in awe of God's magnificent creation. We listen with joy to the sounds of children laughing. We smile at the sight of a family taking the time to enjoy a day at the park. These little things often go unnoticed by people caught up in the busyness of everyday life. They

are always there, though, and we need to slow down enough so that we can start to focus on the life that goes on around us.

Of course, the greatest reason we can think of to be of good cheer is the fact that someday we are going to be with our loved ones again in the presence of Jesus. This thought brings us real joy and happiness. It is a comfort, though, to think about the reality of heaven and how wonderful it is there. We keep ourselves focused on the jobs that God has given us to accomplish here on earth, but we always keep an "eye" on the life that awaits us. Our joy and comfort come from the Son of God, Jesus Christ our Lord and Savior.

*Our joy and comfort come from the Son of God, Jesus Christ our Lord and Savior.*

## From Grief to Glory

Perhaps you are on the road to recovery and healing right now. We know from our own experience that you probably have a lot of questions, questions that many people either don't understand or can't answer. "Is it okay to date again?" "Should I remarry?" "Is it wrong for me to want to move out of the house where my loved one passed away?" These are just a few of the questions that you may have now. There are no clear-cut answers for these questions. The answer is going to depend on you and your personal circumstances. One thing to remember is that you should never feel compelled to replace the loved one you just said good-bye to. No one will ever replace a son, daughter, husband, or wife.

There is nothing wrong with remarrying or having more children, but examine your motives. Filling a void in your life is fine if you long to reestablish a relationship of love that you lost when your loved one went home. However, be careful that you do not remarry or have another child because you think it will in some way replace the lost loved one. Basically, we just want you to examine the motives of your heart in whatever decisions you need to make.

Perhaps you just can't bring yourself to believe that you will ever be truly happy again. In our lives, we have found that happiness will indeed come again, but it takes time—it takes enduring the process before embracing the promise of healing and restoration. We are very happy people today, and we live and love life to the fullest. However, there is something missing—something that was a precious part of our lives. Our daughter is gone, and we cannot change that. We know she is in heaven and that we will see her again someday, and we are comforted by these thoughts. Even though Gabrielle is no longer with us, we still know that life is worth living and that *"the joy of the LORD is* [our] *strength"* (Nehemiah 8:10).

*Happiness will indeed come again, but it takes time.*

Perhaps you have been reading this book and you want to believe all the good promises of God, but you are uncertain of your eternal destiny. Maybe you have determined that Jesus needs to become the central focus of your life and that you want to make sure you spend eternity with Him in heaven. If so, Jesus is ready to come in to your life as your Lord and Savior! If you are

ready to accept Him right now, then pray this prayer out loud:

> "Jesus, I accept you now as my Lord and Savior. I purposefully choose You, Jesus. I know You are the Way, the Truth, and the Life. I ask You to fill my heart with Your love. I know that You are my destiny here on earth and for eternity in heaven. I look forward to the day when I am in Your presence forever. Thank You, Lord. In Jesus' name, amen."

You can be happy again, and you can enjoy life to the fullest as God walks with you from day to day. The greatest advice we can give to you is to seek the wisdom of God for the answers to your questions. He will never mislead you. He wants to see you live a full and abundant life, and He is ready to do whatever He can to help you do that. However, it all starts with you. Don't miss out on the unspeakable joy of life because you let your grief control you. Through the Holy Spirit, God can heal your brokenness, fill your emptiness, and revive your wounded spirit.

*The greatest advice we can give to you is to seek the wisdom of God for the answers to your questions.*

Our hearts go out to those of you who are in the midst of mourning. Our prayers are with you. The process of healing and restoration that God provides will bring renewal to your life. Choose now to embrace the process so that you might enjoy the promise of a new day living in God's love and grace. Go on with the Lord

to the place of peace and joy. Let Him lead you down the path that takes you from grief to glory!

*"Weeping may endure for a night, but joy*
*comes in the morning."*
—Psalm 30:5

## *Points to Ponder*

1.  Write out a prayer in which you affirm your commitment to God and to living for Him every day of your life. Thank Him for the life He has given you, and ask Him to continue to show you the wonder of His *"great love"* (Psalm 17:7 NIV).

2.  If you do not currently keep a journal, prayerfully consider starting one. Writing in a journal on a regular basis is an excellent way to express your feelings, deal with negative thoughts, pour your heart out before the Lord, and reaffirm your faith in God.

# Appendix:

## God's Word to You

Throughout this book, we've included numerous references to Bible passages that can help you stay strong during the grieving process. In this section, you will find several of these Scriptures and others listed according to chapter topics. By doing this, we hope to provide you with a handy reference of verses that can help you deal with emotions you may feel during your times of pain and anguish. May God bless you as you read and ponder His mighty Word!

# *Chapter One*
# *Standing Strong When Tragedy Strikes*

cs *"Behold, I am the* Lord, *the God of all flesh. Is there anything too hard for Me?"* (Jeremiah 32:27)

cs *"Do not be afraid; only believe."* (Mark 5:36)

cs *"Therefore you now have sorrow; but I will see you again and your heart will rejoice, and your joy no one will take from you."* (John 16:22)

cs *"In the world you will have tribulation; but be of good cheer, I have overcome the world."* (John 16:33)

cs *"We are more than conquerors through Him who loved us."* (Romans 8:37)

cs *"I can do all things through Christ who strengthens me."* (Philippians 4:13)

cs *"Fight the good fight of faith."* (1 Timothy 6:12)

# Chapter Two
# Taking the First Steps Back toward Life

ଔ *"You will keep him in perfect peace, whose mind is stayed on You, because he trusts in You."* (Isaiah 26:3)

ଔ *"To comfort all who mourn, to console those who mourn in Zion, to give them beauty for ashes, the oil of joy for mourning, the garment of praise for the spirit of heaviness."* (Isaiah 61:2–3)

ଔ *"Therefore, whatever you want men to do to you, do also to them."* (Matthew 7:12)

ଔ *"Peace I leave with you, My peace I give to you; not as the world gives do I give to you. Let not your heart be troubled, neither let it be afraid."* (John 14:27)

ଔ *"These things I have spoken to you, that My joy may remain in you, and that your joy may be full."* (John 15:11)

ଔ *"God is not the author of confusion but of peace."* (1 Corinthians 14:33)

ଔ *"For we walk by faith, not by sight."* (2 Corinthians 5:7)

ଔ *"Be anxious for nothing, but in everything by prayer and supplication, with thanksgiving, let*

*your requests be made known to God; and the peace of God, which surpasses all understanding, will guard your hearts and minds through Christ Jesus."* (Philippians 4:6–7)

# Chapter Three
## Knowing Your Limits

ଔ *"For you created my inmost being; you knit me together in my mother's womb. I praise you because I am fearfully and wonderfully made; your works are wonderful, I know that full well."* (Psalm 139:13–14 NIV)

ଔ *"He will sit as a refiner and a purifier of silver."* (Malachi 3:3)

ଔ *"Do you not know that your body is the temple of the Holy Spirit?"* (1 Corinthians 6:19)

ଔ *"For ye have need of patience, that, after ye have done the will of God, ye might receive the promise."* (Hebrews 10:36 KJV)

ଔ *"Let patience have its perfect work, that you may be perfect and complete, lacking nothing."* (James 1:4)

# Chapter Four
# Heeding the Voice of the Lord

cs *"Trust in the* Lord *with all your heart, and lean not on your own understanding; in all your ways acknowledge Him, and He shall direct your paths."* (Proverbs 3:5–6)

cs *"Cast your cares on the* Lord *and he will sustain you."* (Psalm 55:22 NIV)

cs *"Ask, and it will be given to you; seek, and you will find; knock, and it will be opened to you. For everyone who asks receives, and he who seeks finds, and to him who knocks it will be opened."* (Matthew 7:7–8)

cs *"Cast all your anxiety on him because he cares for you."* (1 Peter 5:7 NIV)

# Chapter Five
## Learning to Embrace the Process of Pain

cs *"But He knows the way that I take; when He has tested me, I shall come forth as gold."* (Job 23:10)

cs *"No discipline seems pleasant at the time, but painful. Later on, however, it produces a harvest of righteousness and peace for those who have been trained by it. Therefore, strengthen your feeble arms and weak knees. 'Make level paths for your feet,' so that the lame may not be disabled, but rather healed."* (Hebrews 12:11–13 NIV)

cs *"Count it all joy when you fall into various trials, knowing that the testing of your faith produces patience. But let patience have its perfect work, that you may be perfect and complete, lacking nothing."* (James 1:2–4)

cs *"Now for a little while, if need be, you have been grieved by various trials, that the genuineness of your faith, being much more precious than gold that perishes, though it is tested by fire, may be found to praise, honor, and glory at the revelation of Jesus Christ."* (1 Peter 1:6–7)

## Chapter Six
## *Finding Comfort through Emotional Release*

ଓ *"Weeping may endure for a night, but joy comes in the morning."* (Psalm 30:5)

ଓ *"Record my lament; list my tears on your scroll—are they not in your record?"* (Psalm 56:8 NIV)

ଓ *"Those who sow in tears shall reap in joy. He who continually goes forth weeping, bearing seed for sowing, shall doubtless come again with rejoicing, bringing his sheaves with him."* (Psalm 126:5–6)

ଓ *"To everything there is a season, a time for every purpose under heaven:…A time to weep, and a time to laugh; a time to mourn, and a time to dance."* (Ecclesiastes 3:1, 4)

ଓ *"Blessed are those who mourn, for they shall be comforted."* (Matthew 5:4)

## *Chapter Seven*
## *Coping with Mental Anguish*

ເ� *"Two are better than one, because they have a good reward for their labor."* (Ecclesiastes 4:9)

ເ� *"I am the way, the truth, and the life."* (John 14:6)

ເ� *"And I will pray the Father, and He will give you another Helper, that He may abide with you forever."* (John 14:16)

ເ� *To live is Christ, and to die is gain."* (Philippians 1:21)

ເ� *"Whatever things are true, whatever things are noble, whatever things are just, whatever things are pure, whatever things are lovely, whatever things are of good report, if there is any virtue and if there is anything praiseworthy; meditate on these things."* (Philippians 4:8)

ເ� *"Pray for one another, that you may be healed."* (James 5:16)

# Chapter Eight
# Quieting the Voice of the Flesh

cs *"There is therefore now no condemnation to those who are in Christ Jesus, who do not walk according to the flesh, but according to the Spirit."* (Romans 8:1)

cs *"All things work together for good to those who love God, to those who are the called according to His purpose."* (Romans 8:28)

cs *"Be transformed by the renewing of your mind, that you may prove what is that good and acceptable and perfect will of God."* (Romans 12:2)

cs *"For the weapons of our warfare are not carnal but mighty in God for pulling down strongholds, casting down arguments and every high thing that exalts itself against the knowledge of God, bringing every thought into captivity to the obedience of Christ."* (2 Corinthians 10:4–5)

cs *"For we do not wrestle against flesh and blood, but against principalities, against powers, against the rulers of the darkness of this age, against spiritual hosts of wickedness in the heavenly places. Therefore take up the whole armor of God, that you may be able to withstand in the evil day, and having done all, to stand."* (Ephesians 6:12–13)

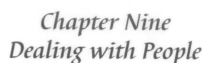
# Chapter Nine
## Dealing with People

ভ *"Death and life are in the power of the tongue, and those who love it will eat its fruit."* (Proverbs 18:21)

ভ *"Love one another. As I have loved you, so you must love one another."* (John 13:34 NIV)

ভ *"Therefore be imitators of God as dear children. And walk in love, as Christ also has loved us and given Himself for us"* (Ephesians 5:1–2)

ভ *"Put on tender mercies, kindness, humility, meekness, longsuffering; bearing with one another, and forgiving one another, if anyone has a complaint against another; even as Christ forgave you, so you also must do."* (Colossians 3:12–13)

ভ *"All of you be submissive to one another, and be clothed with humility, for 'God resists the proud, but gives grace to the humble.'"* (1 Peter 5:5)

# Chapter Ten
## Focusing on What You Still Have

ଓ *"Do not remember the former things, nor consider the things of old. Behold, I will do a new thing, now it shall spring forth."* (Isaiah 43:18–19)

ଓ *"For I know the thoughts that I think toward you, says the LORD, thoughts of peace and not of evil, to give you a future and a hope."* (Jeremiah 29:11)

ଓ *"Blessed be the God and Father of our Lord Jesus Christ, who has blessed us with every spiritual blessing in the heavenly places in Christ."* (Ephesians 1:3)

ଓ *"In Him we have redemption through His blood, the forgiveness of sins, according to the riches of His grace which He made to abound toward us in all wisdom and prudence."* (Ephesians 1:7–8)

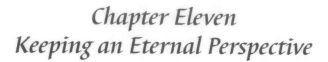
# Chapter Eleven
## Keeping an Eternal Perspective

ॐ *"But seek first the kingdom of God and His righteousness, and all these things shall be added to you. Therefore do not worry about tomorrow, for tomorrow will worry about its own things. Sufficient for the day is its own trouble."* (Matthew 6:33–34)

ॐ *"God, who gives life to the dead and calls those things which do not exist as though they did."* (Romans 4:17)

ॐ *"Set your mind on things above, not on things on the earth."* (Colossians 3:2)

ॐ *"But now they desire a better, that is, a heavenly country. Therefore God is not ashamed to be called their God, for He has prepared a city for them."* (Hebrews 11:16)

# *Chapter Twelve*
# *Recalling the Reward That Awaits*

cs *"You will show me the path of life; in Your presence is fullness of joy; at Your right hand are pleasures forevermore."* (Psalm 16:11)

cs *"But as it is written: 'Eye has not seen, nor ear heard, nor have entered into the heart of man the things which God has prepared for those who love Him.'"* (1 Corinthians 2:9)

cs *"Our citizenship is in heaven."* (Philippians 3:20)

cs *"He who has an ear, let him hear what the Spirit says to the churches. To him who overcomes I will give to eat from the tree of life, which is in the midst of the Paradise of God."* (Revelation 2:7)

# Chapter Thirteen
# Choosing to Live Again

ଔ *"I call heaven and earth as witnesses today against you, that I have set before you life and death, blessing and cursing; therefore choose life, that both you and your descendants may live."* (Deuteronomy 30:19)

ଔ *"'For I know the plans I have for you,' declares the* Lord, *'plans to prosper you and not to harm you, plans to give you hope and a future.'"* (Jeremiah 29:11 NIV)

ଔ *"The joy of the* Lord *is your strength."* (Nehemiah 8:10)

ଔ *"Do you not know that those who run in a race all run, but one receives the prize? Run in such a way that you may obtain it. And everyone who competes for the prize is temperate in all things. Now they do it to obtain a perishable crown, but we for an imperishable crown."* (1 Corinthians 9:24–25)

ଔ *"I press on toward the goal to win the prize for which God has called me heavenward in Christ Jesus."* (Philippians 3:14 NIV)

# Additional Scriptures about Heaven

cs *"And the ransomed of the Lord shall return, and come to Zion with singing, with everlasting joy on their heads. They shall obtain joy and gladness, and sorrow and sighing shall flee away."* (Isaiah 35:10)

cs *"Do not lay up for yourselves treasures on earth, where moth and rust destroy and where thieves break in and steal; but lay up for yourselves treasures in heaven, where neither moth nor rust destroys and where thieves do not break in and steal."* (Matthew 6:19–20)

cs *"For the Son of Man will come in the glory of His Father with His angels, and then He will reward each according to his works."* (Matthew 16:27)

cs *"His lord said to him, 'Well done, good and faithful servant; you were faithful over a few things, I will make you ruler over many things. Enter into the joy of your lord.'"* (Matthew 25:21)

cs *"Then he said to Jesus, 'Lord, remember me when You come into Your kingdom.' And Jesus said to him, 'Assuredly, I say to you, today you will be with Me in Paradise.'"* (Luke 23:42–43)

cs *"For God so loved the world that He gave His only begotten Son, that whoever believes in Him should not perish but have everlasting life."* (John 3:16)

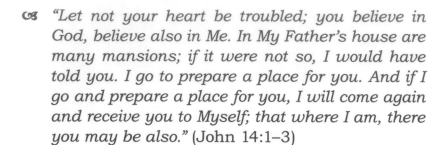

ଔ *"Let not your heart be troubled; you believe in God, believe also in Me. In My Father's house are many mansions; if it were not so, I would have told you. I go to prepare a place for you. And if I go and prepare a place for you, I will come again and receive you to Myself; that where I am, there you may be also."* (John 14:1–3)

ଔ *"For I consider that the sufferings of this present time are not worthy to be compared with the glory which shall be revealed in us."* (Romans 8:18)

ଔ *"They shall neither hunger anymore nor thirst anymore; the sun shall not strike them, nor any heat; for the Lamb who is in the midst of the throne will shepherd them and lead them to living fountains of waters. And God will wipe away every tear from their eyes."* (Revelation 7:16–17)

ଔ *"And God will wipe away every tear from their eyes; there shall be no more death, nor sorrow, nor crying. There shall be no more pain, for the former things have passed away."* (Revelation 21:4)

ଔ *"There shall be no night there: They need no lamp nor light of the sun, for the Lord God gives them light. And they shall reign forever and ever."* (Revelation 22:5)

ଔ *"And behold, I am coming quickly, and My reward is with Me, to give to every one according to his work."* (Revelation 22:12)

*Gabrielle Christian Salem*

# Contact Information:

## Salem Family Ministries

P.O. Box 701287

Tulsa, OK 74170

(918) 369-8008

e-mail: info@salemfamilyministries.org

website: www.salemfamilyministries.org

*For other books by Harry and Cheryl Salem,
visit their website or your local bookstore.*

# ANOTHER POWERFUL *B*OOK

## from Whitaker House

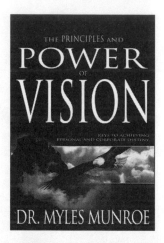

### The Principles and Power of Vision
*Dr. Myles Munroe*

Whether you are a businessperson, a homemaker, a student, or a head of state, author Myles Munroe explains how you can make your dreams and hopes a living reality. Your success is not dependent on the state of the economy or what the job market is like. You do not need to be hindered by the limited perceptions of others or by a lack of resources. Discover time-tested principles that will enable you to fulfill your vision no matter who you are or where you come from. You were not meant for a mundane or mediocre life. Revive your passion for living, pursue your dream, discover your vision—and find your true life.

ISBN: 0-88368-951-0 • Hardcover • 240 pages

### Available at Your Local Christian Bookstore
Visit our website at: www.whitakerhouse.com

from Whitaker House

### How to Stop the Pain

*Dr. James B. Richards*

You've been wounded, and you just can't seem to heal. You forgive, but you can't forget! This paradigm-shattering book will free you from the forces that would turn you into a victim. It will lead you step-by-step through a simple process that will free you from the pain of the past and protect you from the pain of the future.

ISBN: 0-88368-722-4 • Trade • 208 pages

**Available at Your Local Christian Bookstore**
Visit our website at: www.whitakerhouse.com

# ANOTHER POWERFUL *B*OOK
## from Whitaker House

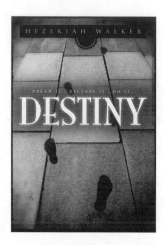

### Destiny: Dream It, Declare It, Do It!
*Hezekiah Walker*

Everyone was born with gifts, talents, desires, and dreams. Yet when many people look at themselves and their lives, they see nothing but the impossible. The passion that once burned deep inside them seems to have all but died. Fear of the future or pain from the past paralyzes their ability to pursue their dreams. Don't let your destiny slip through your fingers like so many others who have carried their dreams to the grave! Step out in faith, and join Hezekiah Walker as he challenges you to achieve your destiny—just dream it, declare it, and do it!

ISBN: 0-88368-874-3 • Trade • 176 pages

## Available at Your Local Christian Bookstore
### Visit our website at: www.whitakerhouse.com

# OTHER POWERFUL BOOKS

## from Whitaker House

### The Hidden Kingdom
*Dr. Dale A. Fife*

There are divine moments in life when you turn a corner and are astounded by unexpected, breathtaking vistas that you never imagined. Suddenly your world is changed forever. You have entered a supernatural realm, an eternal dimension, where Jesus is Lord and creation itself shouts His glory. The brilliantly illuminating revelation in *The Hidden Kingdom* will catapult you into such an experience. If you want an empowered life, this book will lead you on a journey into the heart of God.

ISBN: 0-88368-947-2 • Trade • 256 pages

### The Secret Place
*Dr. Dale A. Fife*

You hunger to live in the presence of God. You yearn to know the Father's heart in an intimate way. You desire revelation and passionate encounters with the Almighty. You want to spend time away from the world, getting to know the Father in a deeper way. If you long to experience a greater intimacy with the Father, *The Secret Place* will draw you in and change your life!

ISBN: 0-88368-715-1 • Trade • 240 pages

**Available at Your Local Christian Bookstore**
Visit our website at: www.whitakerhouse.com

D0001405